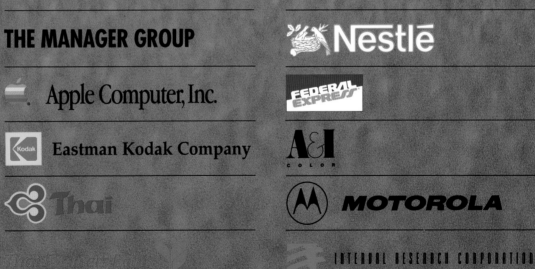

Pedro Coll

This project was made possible through the generous assistance of:

THE MANAGER GROUP

Apple Computer, Inc.

Eastman Kodak Company

Thai

the Regent BANGKOK

Nestlé

FEDERAL EXPRESS

A&I COLOR

MOTOROLA

INTERVAL RESEARCH CORPORATION

With the additional assistance of:

SuperMac Technology
Tamron Industries, Inc.
Xerox Corporation

Barry Lewis

Page 1: In Bac Thai province, women rake weeds from rice paddies. Photo by Pedro Coll, Spain

Pages 2-3: On a tributary of the Bach Dang River in Quang Ninh Province, in northeastern Vietnam, a lone boatman ferries a precious cargo: rich, moist clay, used to make bricks. Photo by Barry Lewis, United Kingdom

Pages 4-5: Following centuries of footsteps, a group of Hmong farmers in Lao Cai Province head off for work in the early morning mist. Photo by Jay Dickman, USA

Pages 6-7: Young boys crouch atop Chinese tombs near Ho Chi Minh City (Saigon). Photo by Basil Pao, Hong Kong

Pages 8-9: The waters off of the coast of Mui Ne, a seaside village in Binh Thuan Province, are teeming with squid, crab, and striped mullet. When the weather warms up, the season will resume, and the village fleet will head out to sea. Photo by Natalie Fobes, USA

Pages 10-11: Millions of Vietnamese live along the country's thousands of canals and waterways. In the city of Hue, the Perfume River gently rocks the home of a young family. Photo by Monica Almeida, USA

Portions of Peter Saidel's essay "Portrait of Change" originally appeared in the San Francisco Examiner.

Published by
Against All Odds Productions
& Melcher Media

Library of Congress Cataloging-in-Publication Data

Smolan, Rick and Jennifer Erwitt

Passage to Vietnam/by Rick Smolan and Jennifer Erwitt
ISBN 1-885559-00-3

94-071853
CIP

Designed by Thomas K. Walker, GRAF/x

Printed in Hong Kong

10 9 8 7 6 5 4 3 2 1

First Edition

PASSAGE TO VIETNAM

THROUGH THE EYES OF SEVENTY PHOTOGRAPHERS

Created by Rick Smolan and Jennifer Erwitt
Designed by Thomas K. Walker

Produced by
AGAINST ALL ODDS PRODUCTIONS
in association with
MANAGER SMOLAN MILLET

Published by
AGAINST ALL ODDS PRODUCTIONS
& MELCHER MEDIA

THE NIGHT I ARRIVED IN VIETNAM, A FRIEND AND I DECIDED TO GO OUT FOR dinner. The way you get around Hanoi and many other Vietnamese cities is to hail a *cyclo*, a bicycle with a seat attached to the front. For about 50 cents a cyclo driver will take you anywhere you want to go. My friend and I each hailed our own cyclo, jumped in, and in a moment, we were off, flying down Le Thai To Street.

People, bicycles, scooters, jeeps, ox carts, trucks, and animals jammed the streets and everything was softened by a dusky light. On the sidewalks and in hundreds of narrow doorways we passed families sitting down to lantern-lit dinners. Children, teenagers, parents, and grandparents were gathered together around televisions on the sidewalk. Fruit and bean sellers, bare light bulbs dangling over their carts, beckoned to us. A few people looked up and smiled as they saw our foreign faces go whizzing by.

The first time we entered a four-way intersection, I braced myself for a collision. There were no traffic signs or signals, and everyone was barreling full speed into the crossing. We headed straight for a woman on a bicycle cradling an infant under her arm. And then something happened. Halfway through the intersection everyone suddenly seemed to obey some set of rules that my companion and I could only guess at. We emerged unscathed out the other side of the crossing and sped onward through the darkening Hanoi streets, past the ornate Beaux-Arts Opera House, past old French mansions, with a receding sense of panic and a growing sense of awe. My companion's driver drew his cyclo alongside mine. My friend leaned over and whispered, "Rick, this is the best damn fifty-cent ride I've ever had!"

That first impression of Vietnam stays with me, even after all these months, because on that brief cyclo ride the images of Vietnam I'd brought with me began to change. In those short ten minutes, my preconceptions of a grim, war-ravaged land, fed by memories of news footage from 25 years ago, were swept away. In the next few weeks I discovered how different this country was, not only from its own troubled past, but from any place that I had ever been. It was as if someone had lifted a curtain and behind it was old Asia: exotic, mysterious, and remarkably photogenic.

I began my career as a photojournalist over twenty years ago, working in Asia, and I have been fortunate to work side by side with some of the most talented photojournalists in the world. One of the things that excited me the most about organizing *Passage to Vietnam* was being able to give this international group men and women, who each day serve as the world's eyes, the opportunity to experience Vietnam for themselves.

Vietnam is a country in transition, a nation that is emerging from a long isolation and making up fast for lost time. As you turn the pages of this book, I hope you will find yourself on your own passage of understanding. And, like the 70 photographers who spread across Vietnam for one week, I hope you will be changed by what you see.

Rick Smolan

ONE

DREAMS
OF A
GENTLE LAND

BY PICO IYER

L IKE MOST TROPICAL COUNTRIES, VIETNAM GETS UP WITH THE light, and one of the greatest pleasures you can find is to go outside at six in the morning and see the whole town out stretching its limbs, playing badminton or soccer in the streets, ghosting its way through *tai chi* motions.

And for all the bullet holes that scar the country, the foreigner has only to say he's from America, and he is greeted with shiningly genuine smiles. "For us, French is the language of power and love," a Vietnamese friend explained. "English is the language of commerce. Russian is the language of quarrels." The only preparation an American need make if going to Vietnam today is to free his mind of preconceptions and images: the only things he need fear are an excess of curiosity and goodwill (and the insults of children who mistake him for a Soviet).

It is hard, in fact, not to grow woozily romantic when enumerating the holiday seductions of the land. There are mist-wreathed rain forests in the west and north, where you can find 53 distinct minority tribes—each with its own colorful costume, customs, and tongue—hunting, still, with bows and arrows. There are atmospheric old French villas, peeling behind coconut palms and green gates, made more nostalgic now by decay, and lined by lovely avenues of tamarind. There are illuminated lanterns and oil-lit lamps along the crooked streets at night, which take you back to the Indochina of your dreams, and the urbane pleasures of white-linen restaurants serving mandarin juice and coq au vin while serenading you with piano and violin duets. There are 1,400 miles of coastline stud-

Cargo is moved from sampan to rowboat on a tributary of the Red River Delta in Ninh Binh Province. Photo by Elliott Erwitt, USA

ded with deserted pure-white beaches, and there are prices that are extravagantly low (huge reproductions of 136 masterpieces from the Hermitage Museum in St. Petersburg can be had for a dollar, and a tube of lipstick for 10 cents).

Most of all, though, there are the exceptionally attractive, cultured, and hospitable people, who still light up at the sight of foreigners, yet who are still self-possessed and full of a quick intelligence—for which they have long been famous. "The Vietnamese are the last natural human people in the world," a well-traveled businessman told me with a touch of hyperbole, perhaps, over drinks in Hanoi.

Yet the real attraction of Vietnam today comes from something deeper. When we choose a place to visit, the way a country carries itself and markets itself—the way it knows itself, really—is everything. We flee certain resorts not just because they are touristed but more because they have begun to see themselves through tourists' eyes, to amend themselves to tourists' needs, to carry themselves in capital letters; because, in short, they have simplified themselves into their sense of what a foreigner wants.

In the harbor of Phan Thiet, a fishing village in Binh Thuan Province, these women have their own catches in mind: customers looking for something to eat. These boats carry hot charcoal stoves and utensils used to prepare soups and baguette *sandwiches for departing fishermen. Photo by Natalie Fobes, USA*

Farmers use sampans to take their rice to market in Camau, Minh Hai Province. Photo by Michael S. Yamashita, USA

One-year-old Nguyen Tho cries for his mother, who is busy harvesting rice near the village of Trung An in Tien Giang Province.
Photo by Nguyen Duy Anh, Vietnam

On a mist-shrouded path near Tam Dao, a town in Vinh Phu Province, villagers walk to the local market. Refrigerators are rare in Vietnam, so most women make at least one trip to the market every day of the week.
Photo by Vu Nhat, Vietnam

None of this is true—yet—of Vietnam, which still has the bashful charm of a naturally alluring girl stepping out into bright sunlight after years of dark seclusion. Protected, ironically, by its years of hardship and cut off from modernity by almost two decades of communist rule, Vietnam is still, more than most places, new to the world. It does not know what to make of us, nor we of it. Its pleasures feel unrehearsed, and surprise is still a growth industry there.

That is one reason, of course, why everyone seems to be converging on it—Bangkok-based stockbrokers, Japanese businessmen, even the photographers in this book—all eager to grab a piece of the hidden treasure before it splinters or corrodes. Vietnam feels very much like the coming thing, the next "little dragon," tomorrow's hot destination: a perfect locale, indeed, for the kinder, greener, post-Cold War '90s. It is already becoming a crossroads of the fashionable: In my hotel in Hanoi, an assistant producer from the French production company, Paradis Films, was bargaining over a suite for Catherine Deneuve; and when I went to the Cao Dai church in Tay Ninh, the name above mine in the visitor's book was that of Gough Whitlam, former Prime Minister of Australia.

For the moment, though, the country's facilities are still, thankfully, uncertain. Some hotels in Vietnam offer elevators, some have watercoolers, some have girls who slip into your room the minute you return from dinner. Some have Viettronics shortwave radios in each room; some, high-tech phones so complex they cannot even reach the front desk; some, caged monkeys in their gardens. In one deluxe hotel I stayed in, keys were scattered across the reception desk so that any guest could effectively take the key to any room (communal property indeed!). In another, ubiquitous signs warned, "Pets, Fire Arms, Explosives, Inflamables, and Stinking Things Are Not Allowed in the Hotel." In still another, I went into my room one day to find a chambermaid cadging a free shower.

Vietnam is also the kind of place where restaurants offer armadillo and cobras slaughtered at your table; artichoke tea, gecko-steeped liqueurs and—the specialty of Dalat—coffee made from beans vomited up by a weasel. It is a place where beer costs more than wine, and a Coke more than an entire meal.

It is also a place where traveling by car means bumping along Highway 1, through a confusion of bicycles shrouded in brushes and brooms, buses piled high with tail-wagging dogs, and horse-drawn carts, at speeds no faster than 10 m.p.h., over "elephant holes" that put out the backs of any foreigners who are not banging their heads against the roofs, and where, after nightfall, the only lights one sees are reflections in the eyes of passing water buffalo. The alternative— taking the local airline—may not be any happier. On my flight, all the seats in the back two rows were different colors, the portholes were guarded by flimsy curtains, and the back third of the aircraft—a former Soviet military plane—was an empty space with trays of meatballs stacked on the floor (and later handed out by a phlegmatic teenage boy). The whole place had the air of a hospital waiting-room in the clouds.

Insofar as any Marxism is to be found in Vietnam, Hanoi, of course, is the place; yet even in the capital it is hardly strident or insistent. Groups of peasants from the countryside troop all day long around the Ho Chi Minh Museum,

The Hmong, one of Vietnam's 53 ethnic minorities, cluster in Lao Cai Province in the northwestern highlands. The black scarves and indigo aprons worn by these three young women—photographed while preparing soil for rice-planting—identify them as Black Hmong, one of a half-dozen subgroups. Other Hmong clans include the Green, whose women let their hair fall freely to the shoulders, and the White, who wear unbleached fabric and shave most of the hair from their heads.

The first travelers to journey to this part of the world christened these mountain tribes meo, supposedly because their spoken language reminded the visitors of cats.

There is no written version of this high-pitched language. Hmong traditions are passed orally from one generation to the next.
Photo by Jay Dickman, USA

In every part of Vietnam, planting trees has become a springtime custom, born of Ho Chi Minh's strong belief in their beauty and ecological soundness. This line of shade trees help support the banks of a dike along a road in the My Duc District of Ha Tay Province. Photo by Patrick Tehan, USA

The stilts and thatched roof of this house in rural Hoa Binh Province identify its builders as White Thais. Ethnically and linguistically related to the inhabitants of Thailand, the Vietnamese Thai minority retains its own culture and traditions. Their ancestors settled in the hills of northern Vietnam around the 11th century, A.D. Photo by Guido Alberto Rossi, Italy

but the main item of interest for them may well be the corner that features a Coke sign, a plaster-cast Packard, and Don McCullin's photo of a shell-shocked grunt.

And in any case, the nominal principles of the Party are contradicted all day long by a cacophony of deals. Everywhere seems a marketplace in Hanoi, and every street is bubbling over with free trade: one block given over to a stack of black-and-white TVs, another to a rack of bicycles. In another block, 30 barbers are lined up with their backs to traffic, their mirrors set along the wall before them. Old men puff Hero and Gallantes cigarettes over pyramids of Nescafé bottles, bookshops explode with stacks of Madonna fan mags. In the covered market, US$15-a-kilo turtles and fat snakes sit next to "Maradona Jeans" caps and shirts with "One Hundred Dollars" printed on them. And out on the streets, the stalls are loaded with knockoff Casios, Disney T-shirts, Snoopy bags, and pills guaranteed to save one from "addiction to narcotics." An absence of external resources is more than made up for by inner: A teacher in Vietnam earns US$9 a month, yet half the households in the country, according to my guide, have VCRs.

All this is why Vietnam is changing before one's very eyes—and anyone who saw Bangkok or Beijing eight years ago and revisits either place today knows that Eastern cities can take off with the urgency of a Chinese firecracker. Ever since the government in Hanoi decided to open up the country to free trade and private enterprise several years ago, the famous energy and enterprise of the Vietnamese have been transforming the country at the speed of light. And now, as relations are finally normalized with Washington, the boom-town electricity of the country feels more palpable than ever: as if much of Vietnam were letting out its breath, in a great gust of relief, after years—and years—of holding it in.

Spindly crosswalks reach over a canal network in the Delta province of An Giang. Known as monkey bridges, in tribute to the agility of those who use them, these makeshift walkways are constructed from skeins of mangrove and bamboo, lashed together with vines. In recent years, some of them have been torn down in the name of progress and replaced by concrete pedestrian overpasses.

Photo by Michael S. Yamashita, USA

THE TRAIN BETWEEN HANOI AND HAIPHONG,
loaded with passengers on their way to market, slows
to a halt. Most of Vietnam's railroad network was built
during the French colonial era. Today, more than 100
steam engines are still in service. On local lines like
this one, "hard seat" is the only class available.
Photo by Bruno Barbey, France

ON THE REUNIFICATION EXPRESS, THE kitchen staff shells eggs with scant concern for flying cigarette ash. The 1,072-mile line connects Hanoi and Ho Chi Minh City (Saigon), with stops in Danang, Hue, and other major cities. Under ideal conditions, the trip takes 42 hours, but because the Express is sometimes forced to share the track with slower trains— some of them traveling in the opposite direction—it often takes much longer. To reopen the route after the war, Vietnam had to repair 1,334 bridges, 27 tunnels, and 1,300 switches.
Photo by Misha Erwitt, USA

THE BLACK HMONG HAVE CULTIVATED RICE
in the highlands of Lao Cai Province for several centuries. Five-year-old Vang A Su uses a man-size hoe to break ground for a new terrace, while his father takes a cigarette break.
Photo by Jay Dickman, USA

Pilgrims and tourists head up the Swallow River to the Perfume Pagoda. Photo by Bruno Barbey, France

PILGRIMAGE TO
THE PERFUME PAGODA

Built into the limestone cliffs of the Mountain of the Fragrant Traces, the Perfume Pagoda is one of Vietnam's most popular pilgrimage destinations. Thirty-seven miles southwest of Hanoi, *Chua Huong,* as it is known, draws hundreds of thousands of visitors every year. The peak season comes in late March—when *Passage to Vietnam* photographers Patrick Tehan and Bruno Barbey arrived—as the Vietnamese celebrate the arrival of spring.

The trip begins in the town of Ben Duc, where 2,000 small rowboats wait for pilgrims along the banks of the Swallow River. From there, it is an hour's trip upstream and a mile-long hike to a complex of temples thick with incense and crowded with Buddhist shrines. The primary temple is, in fact, a gigantic cavern, in

Oarsmen await fares at Ben Duc. Photo by Bruno Barbey, France

Pilgrims place envelopes of faux money into flames inside the grotto. The money is intended to help the spirits of ancestors in the afterlife. Photo by Patrick Tehan, USA

Visitors reach for drops of water falling from a stalactite. Symbolic of mother's milk, the water is believed to possess special healing powers. Photo by Patrick Tehan, USA

which many of the stalactites and stalagmites have been painted as religious figures. According to legend, it was here that a Hindu bodhisattva transformed himself into female form, the Goddess of Compassion, known as *Quan Am.*

The huge crowds are a relatively new development. It was only in the late 1980s that Vietnamese society opened up and domestic travel became much easier. One of the results has been a boom in tourism, fueled by a new middle class which has been able to accumulate spending money under the economic reforms. Indeed, the rather steep US$1.40 admission fee (US$6.50 for foreigners) is something that many Vietnamese cannot afford.

Unfortunately, the pagoda is starting to suffer from the resulting wear and tear. During the spring festival, as many as 30,000 people show up on a single day, and the mountain path—already quite smooth after several centuries of foot traffic—becomes difficult to negotiate. Bottlenecks are very common, and many visitors, unable to squeeze through the crowds, turn back before reaching the top.

For those who do make it, the reward is a chance to burn *ma,* or paper offerings to the spirits of deceased relatives. The Vietnamese believe that they are responsible for taking care of their loved ones in the afterlife. Thus, *Ma* can come in the form of *faux* money, paper clothing and even cardboard Sony stereos and refrigerators. The shape of the offering is often determined by what the living think their deceased relative can use best. A woman who died in the 1930s, for example, might receive a traditional *ao dai,* while a teenager who died in the 1980s might get a pair of paper Reeboks.

After their visit to the main temple, many Vietnamese go to pray in the shrine's other grottoes, which are believed to be inhabited by deities who can heal sorrows and purify souls. Afterwards, the visitors will nap, picnic, and relax with friends, before making the arduous journey back down the mountain path.

Monk Thich Dao Sinh stands sentinel in the Perfume Pagoda's main cavern. Photo by Patrick Tehan, USA

IN THE HEART OF HANOI'S OLD TOWN, (*previous page*) the tattered, yet picturesque remnant of a 15th-century walled city, two flower sellers take shelter on Sandworm Shop Street. Like the quarter's 35 other streets, or *pho*, Sandworm Shop Street is named for a craft or product. Some of the tiny streets, like Silk Shop Street, continue to offer their namesakes, as do streets nearby selling everything from ropes to rubber, and gold to gravestones. Many products once sold in the quarter, like sandworms (enjoyed as a delicacy with duck eggs), are no longer in great demand. Their place has been taken up by entirely new lines of goods, like Russian watches, plastic kitchenware, wind-up G.I. Joes, made-in-Korea luggage, and T-shirts, and baseball caps emblazoned with Heineken, Tin Tin, The Doors, and other such logos.

The neighborhood is now threatened by real estate developers who see inefficiency in the neighborhood's narrow streets, red-tiled buildings, mysterious alleyways, and never-ending bustle. They say that the quarter's dilapidation makes it ripe for demolition, while conservationists hope that Vietnam will favor renovating this charming link to the past.
Photo by Nicole Bengiveno, USA

GECKO LIZARDS ARE SOLD BY THE squirming kilo at a market in Phan Rang, Ninh Thuan Province. Dipped in batter and pan-fried, they are a popular specialty in local restaurants. Photographer Torin Boyd likened them to fishsticks, only crunchier.
Photo by Torin Boyd, USA

IN CHOLON, HO CHI MINH CITY'S CHINATOWN, shoppers can choose how they want their ducks to arrive on the dinner table. Some prefer to tie the bird to the handlebars of their bicycles and take it home alive. For an additional fee, the seller will slaughter and feather the evening meal on the spot.
Photo by Radhika Chalasani, USA

THE OPEN-AIR MARKET IN DALAT HAS THE WIDEST variety of foods to be found in Vietnam. In addition to meat, wines, teas, and jams, local merchants sell all manner of produce: garlic, chili, watermelon, custard apples, jackfruits, guavas, and durians, to name a few. *Photo by Mark S. Wexler, USA*

TRADITIONAL NOODLE SOUP, CALLED *PHO*,
is enjoyed by Vietnamese at all hours of the day,
but it is particularly popular for breakfast. The
dish gets its name from the Vietnamese
mispronunciation of the French word *feu*, as in
pot au feu. In downtown Hanoi, soup-stand
owner Do Thi Ha, one of the city's thousands
of *pho* chefs, flavors her broth with prawns,
boiled bones, ginger, and *nuoc mam*, a
fermented fish sauce. She will then add thin,
freshly boiled rice noodles, greens, and
chicken, beef, or pork. Seasoning—hot chili,
lime, salt, and pepper—is left to customers to
add, according to their own tastes.
Photo by Nicole Bengiveno, USA

FOOD AND INCENSE OFFERINGS TO A
deceased relative are prepared on a beach
on Hon Dau Island, a fifteen-minute
boat ride from Haiphong. They will be
placed on the altar of a nearby Buddhist
temple as part of an observance of the
anniversary of the family member's death.
The spirit of the deceased, it is believed,
will consume the essence of the food.
At the end of the ceremony, the living will
eat the food themselves, thereby sharing
a meal with their lost loved one.
Photo by P.F. Bentley, USA

The Vietnamese diet includes the meat of some animals most Westerners would regard as pets. Dog, snake, or turtle can be found on some menus, while monkeys are a rare (and therefore expensive) delicacy. Monkeys at Hanoi's Dong Xuan Market sell for approximately US$300. *Photo by Denise Rocco, USA*

THIS HANOI SHOPKEEPER, PHOTOGRAPHED
at Cho Mo Market during her lunch break,
sells French-style caps, raingear, and rolls of
firecrackers. Her best-selling items—pith
helmets—remain popular in the north because
they are durable, inexpensive, and evoke the
image of the victorious army.
Photo by Bruno Barbey, France

A LOAD OF FISHTRAPS GETS A LIFT ACROSS
the Dap Cau Bridge in Ha Bac Province.
Photo by Gueorgui Pinkhassov, France

AT A CHINESE PAGODA IN CAN THO,
Tang Hai, 81, makes an offering of burning incense. Ethnic Chinese, or Viet Hoa, are Vietnam's largest minority, comprising about 2 percent of the population. Though intermarriage is more common than it used to be, the business acumen of the Viet Hoa, and their suspected ties with China, Vietnam's long-time enemy, have strained their relationship with ethnic Vietnamese.
Photo by Harry Gruyaert, Belgium

AS PART OF AN ANNUAL THREE-DAY CELEBRA-tion honoring a local war hero, a water buffalo is slaughtered, scorched, and bathed in its own blood. The animal, as well as a pig that has been similarly prepared, will be prostrated before the altar of a nearby temple. Villages have honored their illustrious citizens in this manner for centuries. The valiant officer being feted here served under Emperor Minh Mang, who reigned from 1820 to 1840.

Photo by Sarah Leen, USA

BUDDHIST NUNS NORMALLY KEEP THEIR
heads covered, but these women have removed
their hoods and scarves in order to chant and
pray before a vegetarian meal at Su Nu Pagoda
in Dalat. A shaven head symbolizes a woman's
renunciation of vanity, part of a life that rejects
many of the world's material concerns. The
35 residents of the pagoda sleep twelve to
a room; they rise at 3 a.m. for meditation and
prayer, then do chores until sunrise. Work
is organized in shifts, so that responsibility for
cooking and washing dishes is shared by all.
Lunch comes at 11:30, followed by an afternoon of work in the tea fields, from which the
pagoda derives a small income.
Photo by Stephanie Maze, USA

CASTING NETS FROM ATOP BAMBOO STILTS
allows fishermen *(following page)* to avoid
the sharp rocks beneath the surf along the coast
in Nam Ha Province. The method demands
extraordinarily strong legs and, apparently,
a great sense of balance.
Photo by Nguyen Dan, Vietnam

COAL IS MINED BY HAND ALONG THE
northern coast of Quang Ninh Province and
then carried in 100-pound loads across the
beach. Says British photographer Barry Lewis:
"The levels to which people are used, whole
families sometimes, rather than machines, is
frightening. They dynamite the coal, and use
heavy excavators, but then they lift and break
it by hand. They sort it by hand. They shake it
up by hand to get different grades. I saw 50
miners in one section and it was often hard to
tell whether they were men or women because
of the coal dust." Lewis found the child miners
easier to identify—because of their size.

Elsewhere on the beach, the unemployed
dug six feet down into the sand, searching
for undiscovered scraps to sell at 25 cents per
100 pounds. Other families waded in a nearby
river, stooping into the black water. Recalls
Lewis, "My guide said, 'Oh, they're shrimp
fishing.' They weren't. They were trying to find
bits of coal."

Photo by Barry Lewis, United Kingdom

RUSHING TO BEAT NIGHTFALL OVER THE
Mekong, a woman throws her whole body
weight behind the oars. Behind her the lights
are coming on in Can Tho, the Delta's
unofficial capital. By the time it reaches
Vietnam, the 2,000-mile Mekong has divided
into two separate channels which the Vietnamese call Tien Giang (Upper River) and
Hau Giang (Lower River). Can Tho sits on the
latter. At one time, the river split into nine
tributaries before emptying into the South
China Sea, or, as the Vietnamese prefer to call
it, the Eastern Sea. Over the years, two of the
tributaries have silted up, but the Vietnamese
believe the number nine to be auspicious, and
still call the river *Cuu Long,* or Nine Dragons.
Photo by Harry Gruyaert, Belgium

MADE FROM BAMBOO, *THUYEN THUNG,* **OR**
"bucket boats," are used in shallow waters up
and down the Vietnamese coastline. These
two were spotted in the village of Cua Lo, in
Nghe An Province.
Photo by Tara Sosrowardoyo, Indonesia

Near the village of Mui Ron,
Quang Binh Province.
Photo by Tara Sosrowardoyo, Indonesia

A tourist sampan on the Perfume River
in Hue *(left and above)* provides both home
and livelihood for this family. Competition
along the river is tough—hundreds of other
boats vie for the same customers. Photographer
Monica Almeida says she picked this one
because "the woman stood out. She seemed less
aggressive than everybody else."
Photos by Monica Almeida, USA

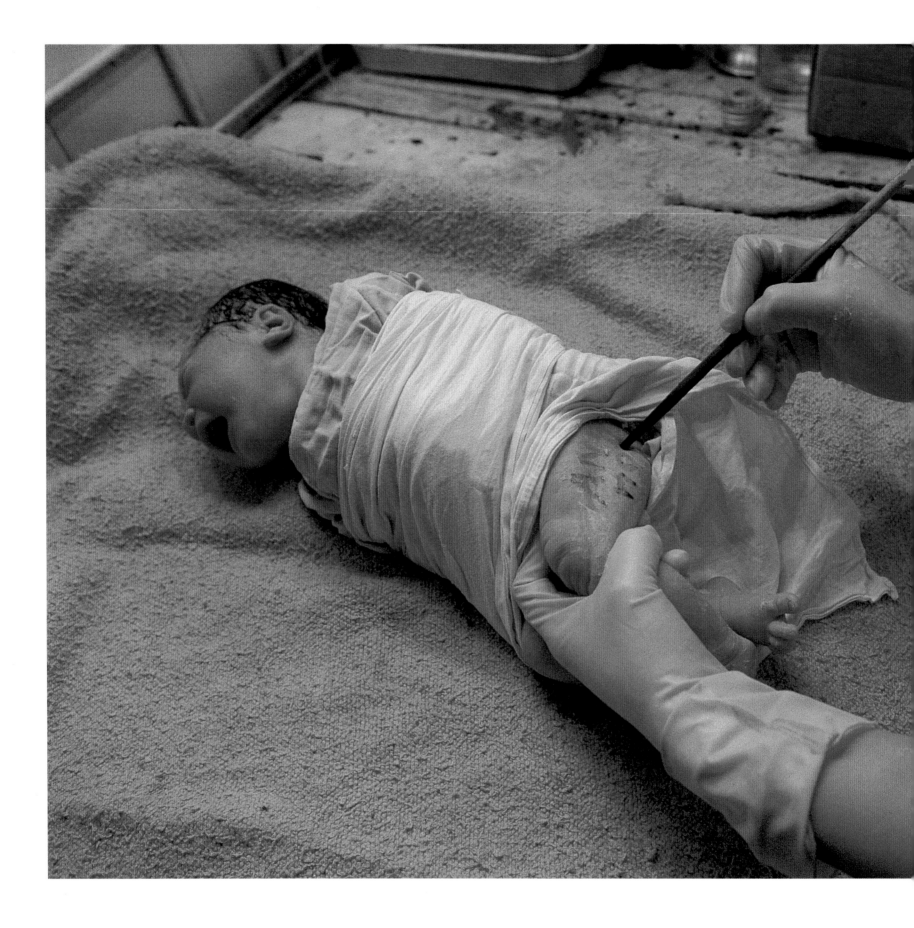

IT COSTS ABOUT 50 CENTS TO HAVE A BABY
at the Institute for the Care of Mothers and the
Newborn in Hanoi. Immediately after birth
(left), the infant's thigh is labeled to guard against
mistaken identities and prevent the swapping
of female babies with male ones. Preference for
males, though not as strong as it used to be, is still
common—intensified, perhaps, by government
pressure on couples to limit themselves to two
children. At the current birthrate, Vietnam's
population will exceed 80 million by the year 2000,
up from the 1992 estimate of 71 million. The
country already has one of the world's youngest
populations: 51.2 percent are under the age
of 21, compared with approximately 33 percent
in the U.S.

An attendant *(above)* listens in on the
heartbeat of an imminent arrival.
Photos by Yann Arthus-Bertrand, France

A Kernel of Rice, God's Gemstone

Vietnamese legend has it that God sent rice to Earth in a magic sack, which he entrusted to a spirit messenger. Before his courier left, God gave him a second magic sack, in which he put grass seeds. "The seeds in the first sack," God said, "will grow when they touch the ground and give a plentiful harvest, anywhere, with no effort. The seeds in the second, however, must be nurtured; but if they are tended properly, they will give the Earth great beauty."

Unfortunately, the spirit messenger got the sacks mixed up. Grass, which humans couldn't eat, became plentiful, while rice, intended by God to feed humankind with little effort, became difficult to cultivate.

Thus the Vietnamese came to accept that feeding themselves would always require back-breaking labor. The process begins in February and July, after the rains. Spread in water-filled patches, the seeds are guarded jealously, protected from birds by children and scarecrows. In 30 to 50 days, they are transplanted into paddies, a job that requires stooping for hours in knee-deep, muddy water. Then, a few months later, the rice is golden brown and ready for harvest. Farmers reap their crop by hand, cutting the stems close to the ground. The leftover stubble is burned, while the best seeds are saved for the cycle to begin again.

This yearly ritual of toil has forged a strong

A team of women plant seedlings in terraced paddies outside the town of Son La in Son La Province. Photo by Pham Tien Dung, Vietnam

Mountains of rice, still in its brown husks, dwarf workers of the Toyo Dragon Rice Factory, in Phung Hiep, Can Tho Province. Photo by Harry Gruyaert, Belgium

At the Toyo Dragon Rice Factory, a joint venture with the Japanese, workers haul rice from beneath the deck of a river barge. Photo by Harry Gruyaert, Belgium

Because wide, flat places are few and far between, roads and highways must serve as drying grounds. Here, on the outskirts of Ho Chi Minh City, a woman spreads out her harvest.
Photo by Radhika Chalasani, USA

bond between the Vietnamese and their most important crop. Every kernel of rice is respected as a symbol of life. Good rice holds a divine status; it is considered God's gemstone, never to be wasted. Even today, parents never strike a child who is eating rice.

Traditionally, the Vietnamese blamed poor harvests on themselves and their lack of piety. But price controls are far more to blame for the disastrous harvests that followed reunification. By the late 1980s, Vietnam could no longer feed itself entirely. Food harvested in the Mekong Delta rotted, marooned by lack of transportation, while in the north people starved.

New policies have lifted most restrictions over farmers, who are now free to enjoy long leases on their land and demand what the market will bear for their produce. Many turn to other crops, but rice remains a staple because of the sustained demand for it. As a result, southern paddies are turning in bumper crops that not only fill Vietnamese stomachs, but have helped turn Vietnam into the world's third biggest exporter, after Thailand and the U.S.

AN UNFINISHED CANAL ON the road to Mui Nai, in Kien Giang Province, is a good place to catch crabs—and enjoy a cooling respite from the hot sun. The ruins of an ancient brick kiln stand in the background.
Photo by Basil Pao, Hong Kong

WEDDING FIREWORKS ATTRACT A GROUP
of school children in Hue. Fireworks—the noisier
and longer-lasting the better—are an essential
component of almost any Vietnamese holiday. At
nuptial celebrations, they greet the bride, drive
off evil spirits, and bring good luck.
Photo by Monica Almeida, USA

A COIL OF FIRECRACKERS IS PACKED WITH gunpowder in Binh Da, a village in Ha Tay Province specializing in their manufacture. Every year during the Tet New Year Festival, villagers compete to produce the biggest, loudest firecrackers.
Photo by Patrick Tehan, USA

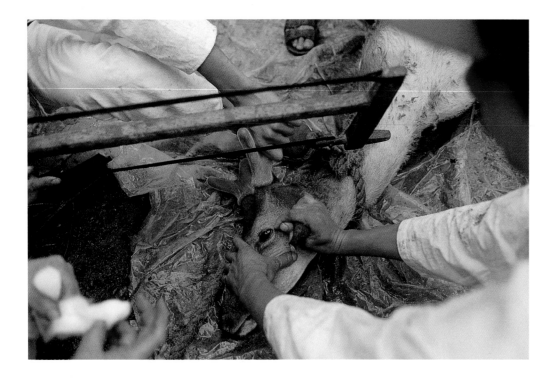

VALUED FOR ITS MEDICINAL PROPERTIES, a pair of antlers, still covered in velvet wrapping, is harvested at a farm on Cat Ba Island. Sliced and simmered with meat or ginseng, antlers are said to cure all kinds of maladies, from bad circulation to impotency. They bring about US$250 a pair—equivalent to an average year's salary for most Vietnamese—from local dealers. The antlers are often sold to importers for much more money in Hong Kong and Taiwan.

Photo by Yann Arthus-Bertrand, France

ACUPUNCTURE IS OFFERED FREE OF CHARGE by Monk Thich Tam Canh every day at 2 p.m. in front of Hanoi's One-Pillar Pagoda. A needle inserted at a point below the elbow treats exhaustion, digestive problems like vomiting and diarrhea, and tennis elbow.
Photo by Joe McNally, USA

71

TWO WORKMEN USE A BENCH TO GET additional leverage from their sawhorse on Cat Ba Island, near Haiphong.
Photo by Yann Arthus-Bertrand, France

IN PREPARATION FOR THE RICE-PLANTING season, a water buffalo drags a plow through the mud near Dong Mo Village, Lang Son Province. Before rice seedlings can be planted, the mud in this field must be churned until it achieves the gooey consistency that one Vietnamese writer compares to soup.
Photo by David Hume Kennerly, USA

A BRICK FACTORY IN HA BAC PROVINCE.
What most impressed French photographer
Gueorgui Pinkhassov about Vietnam was the
motion. "Everyone is working, doing something, going somewhere further, to and fro
endlessly. It was extremely beautiful, this
motion, the unloading of all types of barges,
pulling this and that. It was as if everyone was
dancing, an intricate posing and gesturing."
Photo by Gueorgui Pinkhassov, France

WORKMEN REPAIR A SOVIET-MADE ROCK
grinder at a cement factory in Lang Son, near
the Chinese border. Vietnam is rich in all kinds
of minerals, including coal, semiprecious
gemstones, gold, and forest products, all of
which have caught the eye of foreign investors.
While exports would provide jobs along with
much-needed hard currencies, some Vietnamese worry that all this increased industry will
come at the expense of their country's ecology.
Photo by David Hume Kennerly, USA

AT THE HON KHOI SALT EXPORT FACTORY,
workers flood shallow ponds with sea water,
allowing it to partially evaporate beneath a
scorching sun. The residue, raked into mounds
and carried to the pathways that separate the
ponds, is then heaped into piles *(previous page)*
for collection.

A woman *(left)* spills the harvest onto a
mountain of thick white grains. This photograph is a favorite of American photographer
Karen Kasmauski. "It was terrific," she says. "It
was raining when we first got there, but then
the dark clouds broke up, the workers came out
and the light was perfect. For a few moments I
was blessed." An hour later, everyone was gone.
The same fierce sun that dries the salt makes it
almost impossible to work during the day.
Photos by Karen Kasmauski, USA

NGUYEN THI LU PLANTS RICE SEEDLINGS
(following page) in a cemetery near her village
of Binh Minh in Ha Tay Province, where
the dead lie in expensive tombs or beneath
earthen mounds.

Shortage of land for both planting and
gravesites necessitates their closeness all across
Vietnam. But the proximity sits well with most
Vietnamese because so many of them have
adopted the ancestor worship common to both
Confucianism and Buddhism. Two days in the
country's yearly calendar are set aside for the
dead. The ninth day of the third month is for
"weed pulling of the tombs," a decidedly happy
event rooted in Confucianism. The fifteenth
day of the seventh month, a Buddhist festival,
is dedicated to those who died without
descendants. A nation with such a long history
of war finds solace on both days.
Photo by Patrick Tehan, USA

MOURNING FOR HIS MOTHER, A YOUNG MAN
in Phu Tan Village, Soc Trang Province, bears
her photograph and a cluster of burning joss
sticks, which will help carry her spirit into the
afterlife. High blood pressure prematurely
claimed the life of this 50 year old, who is
survived by a husband, eleven children, and nine
grandchildren. In Vietnam, the average life
expectancy for a woman is 66 years.
Photo by Michael Freeman, United Kingdom

A POLITICIAN'S FUNERAL ON THE OUTSKIRTS
of Hanoi attracts hundreds of well-wishers.
The deceased, Hoang Van Tien, 80, had been the
vice minister at the Ministry of Foreign Affairs.
Though he was entitled to an official state burial,
Tien asked that he be laid to rest in a simple
grave, in his native village of Dinh Bang. One of
Tien's relatives, overcome with grief, is com-
forted by two family members.
Photo by Bruno Barbey, France

Life in a Khmer Buddhist Monastery

Photos by Dilip Mehta

Tranquility and devotion measure the day at the Quy Nong monastery in Tra Vinh Province. Night still blankets the sky when the monastery's twenty novices rise for the day's first prayers. At first light, it's time for chores, after which the monks leave the compound for the outside world, walking in saffron pairs to collect donations of food. The rich and poor Buddhists of the neighboring towns give what they can—keeping the monastery fed affords them the chance to practice the act of *dana*, or "generosity," which, it is believed, will return to them in the future. Back at the monastery, everything is shared, in silence, at a late-morning meal—the only one of the day.

The afternoon is set aside for rest. At 5 p.m., the novices go to their temple for 90 minutes of prayer, during which time they also speak frankly about their thoughts with the monastery elders, in what amounts to a kind of confession. At 9:30 p.m., they return to their dorms to sleep.

The monks, along with 29 percent of the Province's population, are Khmer. As the name implies, their roots are Cambodian, and some Vietnamese Khmer argue that the region rightfully belongs to Cambodia, from which it was seized in the 17th century.

Cambodian culture does live on, however, in the form of Buddhism practiced in the Delta. As in Cambodia, its adherents here claim a greater closeness to original Buddhism, which suggests that Gautama Buddha was a teacher, not a god. This faith, known as Theravada Buddhism, holds that individuals must seek their own salvation. In contrast, followers of the more common Mahayana Buddhism—which is observed in most of Vietnam—believe that Buddha was a deity and that those who have reached enlightenment, known as bodhisattvas, remain in this world to help all beings reach the same transcendent state that they have. Both sects believe in reincarnation, of course, and in an ultimate Nirvana.

THE 3,000 ISLANDS THAT DOT HALONG BAY in Quang Ninh Province are Vietnam's greatest natural wonder, drawing thousands of foreign tourists and Vietnamese each year. Halong, which means "Alighting Dragon," derives its name from a legend that says the region's topography was created by the lashing of a dragon's tail as it made its way from mountain to sea. For a price, fishermen will take you out to search for this same creature, which lives on as Vietnam's version of the Loch Ness monster. *Photo by Yann Arthus-Bertrand, France*

TWO THOUSAND YEARS OF STRUGGLE

BY STANLEY KARNOW

ENERAL VO NGUYEN GIAP, AN ELFIN FIGURE WITH SMOOTH SKIN and white hair, ranks with Grant, Lee, and MacArthur in the pantheon of great commanders. A brilliant strategist, he struggled for 30 years, transforming a handful of ragtag Vietnamese Communist soldiers into an army that routed an expert French force and later defeated a massive American military machine. But he could not have won without the willingness of his troops to make huge sacrifices. The Vietnamese, Giap explained to me in 1990, regard the defense of their homeland as a sacred obligation, and would have paid any price for victory. "Throughout our history," he said, "our profoundest ideology, the pervasive feeling among our people, has been patriotism." Whatever the odds, he would have continued to fight. "Another 20 years, even 100 years, as long as it took to win—regardless of cost."

The Vietnamese forged their sense of nationhood over millennia. Originally from China's Yangtze River valley, they migrated south some 2,000 years ago into the peninsula they now inhabit. China later annexed the territory and built roads, ports, canals and dams to develop its economy. Their schools taught Chinese, which until the French arrived, was the language of the educated. The Vietnamese were also influenced by China's art and architecture. With its curved eaves and inner courtyards, the royal palace in Hue, the former capital of central Vietnam, was modeled on the Forbidden City in Beijing.

But the Vietnamese stubbornly clung to their ethnic identity. They re-

In Cholon, Ho Chi Minh City's Chinatown, a worshipper offers incense at the Thien Hau Pagoda, built by local Cantonese in the early 19th century to honor the Goddess of the Sea. The temple has been lavishly refurbished in recent years by local Chinese, mirroring their revived economic fortunes in Vietnam. Photo by Peter Turnley, USA

peatedly challenged Chinese rule, shaping a warrior tradition that still thrives in their folklore, modern theater, films, and literature. Children pack temples to burn joss sticks and bow to legendary heroes who opposed the Chinese.

In 40 A.D., a noble woman, Trung Trac, along with her sister Nhi, sparked the first of many uprisings against China. They were victorious and established an independent state that stretched from central Vietnam to southern China. After only two years, the Chinese reclaimed the territory, and Trac and Nhi committed suicide by throwing themselves into a river. Another woman, Trieu Au, revolted against the Chinese 200 years later. The Vietnamese Joan of Arc, she wore golden armor as she led her legions from atop an elephant—a scene that to this day is depicted on Vietnamese scrolls, pottery, and cheap souvenirs. Defeated, she also committed suicide, and her defiant words have inspired generations of Vietnamese: "I want to rail against the wind and the tide, kill the whales in the sea, sweep the whole country to save the people from slavery. I refuse to be abused."

Though Vietnam ultimately repulsed China in 1427, it was no less ag-

Among France's bequests to Vietnam is bread, especially baguettes, *shown above as they tumble out of a wood-fired oven in Hoi An, a town in Quang Nam Province. The Vietnamese love to make sandwiches out of all kinds of things, including another French creation, paté, combining it with onions, vegetables, chilis, and ginger.*
Photo by Don Doll, S.J., USA

A former French Air Force officers' club in Ho Chi Minh City now serves as the Ho Chi Minh Community Center. The villa is one of many examples of grand French colonial architecture on Tu Xuong Street. As the uniformed schoolgirls on the steps suggest, this part of town is once again one of the city's finer neighborhoods.
Photo by Catherine Karnow, USA

The founding of the Communist Youth Union is celebrated every year on March 26. While eligibility to join the Union begins during adolescence, recruiting often starts much earlier. As soon as a child enters grade school, he or she may wear the red scarf of the Pioneers, the first stage of becoming a member of the Youth Union. At a time when many vestiges of the communist era are fading, this Union observance in Lang Son Province shows that membership in the Pioneers is still very popular.
Photo by David Hume Kennerly, USA

Whatever his fate in the former satellite states of Eastern Europe, Lenin is still honored in Hanoi, with a statue along Dien Bien Phu Street and a park—the city's largest—that bears his name. Hanoians like to point out that in this sculpture, Vladimir Ilych has his hands over his pockets, a jibe at the cheapskate reputation Russians earned during their years in Vietnam.
Photo by David Alexander, USA

gressive toward its own neighbors. In 1471, the Vietnamese overran Champa, a kingdom located in central Vietnam, whose magnificent brick towers are mute testimony to a forgotten society. They invaded Cambodia and, along with the Thais, would have eventually swallowed up the country had not the French, during their drive into Southeast Asia in the 19th century, protected its integrity. Prince Norodom Sihanouk, the Cambodian chief of state, once told me, "France rescued us from extinction."

By the 19th century, however, Vietnam was no longer focused on expansion. Try as it might, it was unable to keep the French from seizing Saigon, in 1861, and ultimately taking control of all of Indochina, in 1887. Vietnamese who resisted—and there were many—were subjected to "pacification," a euphemism for submission later adopted by the Americans.

The French may have preached liberty, equality, and fraternity, but they summarily jailed and executed dissidents. Some early governors organized opium monopolies that made Vietnam profitable—and turned countless Vietnamese into addicts. French companies ran coal mines, rubber plantations, and other enterprises by exploiting Vietnamese laborers, many of them afflicted with malaria, dysentery, and malnutrition.

Like the British in India, the French tried to mold their colony into an Asian imitation of the home country. The architecture of Hanoi and Ho Chi Minh City bears a distinctly French flavor, while *baguettes* and *crème caramel* can be found on many city streets. Even the alphabet is Roman, created by a French Jesuit, Alexandre de Rhodes, in the 17th century, to replace the Chinese-based ideographs favored by the scholar gentry.

In 1941, Ho Chi Minh, who had been promoting the nationalist cause around the world for decades, decided that the time was ripe for action. He snuck back into Vietnam, where he founded the Vietminh independence movement. Taking advantage of the war raging in the region, he enticed American agents to equip and train his men to harass the Japanese, who had swept the French out in 1940. At the time, he anticipated that the U.S. would later endorse his bid for freedom. But his expectations were dashed.

With World War II over, the French returned to Vietnam, hoping to reconstruct their empire. In 1946, as he braced for a clash, Ho offered a French official an equation that proved to be remarkably accurate: "We will lose ten men for every one you lose, but in the end we will win." In the ensuing war, the U.S. financed the French effort. But the money was spent in vain as the Vietminh, despite severe setbacks, resisted.

Then, in 1953, the French devised a scheme to strike at the Vietminh from a web of garrisons, among them one situated at Dien Bien Phu, a remote valley in the northwest. Giap, after scanning the terrain, recognized that the French would be trapped in their positions. His cannons could pound the French garrison from the surrounding heights while he supplied his battalions from the rear. On March 13, 1954, he attacked, and the French bases fell in rapid order.

By May 7, the red Vietminh flag flew over the the French command bunker. But the Vietminh did not win at the conference table what they had won on the battlefield. At Geneva, the Soviet Union and China, both eager to not antagonize the West, leaned on its Vietnamese allies to agree to divide the country. Pham Van Dong, the senior Vietminh delegate and later North Vietnam's prime

An idiosyncratic amalgam of world religions, the Cao Dai faith traces its origins to the 1920s, when an obscure official working for the French founded the sect as a way to bring Buddhism, Confucianism, and Taoism, Vietnam's main religions, under one God. The doctrine of the faith also borrows from Christianity, Islam, Judaism, and local animism. It holds that the teachings of the leaders of these religions were corrupted by the human frailty of the messengers and their disciples. They believe that certain mortals have managed to see past this corruption to the divine truth. Among these revered mortals are the Chinese revolutionary leader Sun Yat Sen, the French author Victor Hugo, and the Vietnamese poet Nguyen Binh Khiem, whose faces are depicted in a mural in the Great Temple (above left, left to right). Some of the other Westerners on the list: Lenin, Joan of Arc, Louis Pasteur, and Charlie Chaplin. Women pray (above) in the Great Temple of the faith's Holy See, in Long Thanh, Tay Ninh Province. Photos by Péter Korniss, Hungary

Amerasians abandoned in Vietnam have spent two decades adrift, caught between two countries that wanted nothing to do with them. Ignored by the U.S. government, children fathered by Americans were forced to live in a society that is prejudiced against people of mixed blood and regards illegitimate children as socially inferior.

Plus, in the years immediately after the war, anyone associated with America was subjected to extraordinary persecution. Outcasts with little hope for a future, many Amerasians hid on the margins of society, with the other people that the Vietnamese call doi bui, the "dust of life."

Finally, the U.S. began to take notice. The 1987 Homecoming Act gave 30,000 Amerasians

and their immediate families permission to emigrate. Yet a few still remain stuck in limbo. Shortly after American photographer Catherine Karnow photographed Le Thi Bich Lan (left) and Nguyen Thi Kieu Oanh at the Amerasian Transit Center in Ho Chi Minh City, Oanh received permission to emigrate.
Photo by Catherine Karnow, USA

Two slashes appear in the place of the father's name on this Amerasian's birth certificate (right). The Vietnamese consider children who can't trace their bloodlines to be disconnected from the past and hence undesirable as marriage partners. A proverb says that "a child without a father is like a house without a roof." Photo by Karen Kasmauski, USA

minister, subsequently told me, "We were betrayed."

Thus, a separate South Vietnam was created under U.S. auspices. Its president, Ngo Dinh Diem, was a poor choice for the role, despite his nationalist record. He was a Catholic in a predominantly Buddhist country and an aloof bachelor, who cloistered himself in his Saigon palace—as if he were a divine emperor.

Meanwhile, remnants of the Vietminh in the south began to form a small guerrilla force, which a Saigon spokesman dubbed the Vietcong, meaning Vietnamese communist. Though designed to be derisive, the label stuck—so that even the Vietcong would use it. Diem pursued them ruthlessly, arresting thousands and, in many instances, carrying out executions. With only tacit approval from Hanoi, the insurgents fought back. Between 1959 and 1961, assassinations of South Vietnamese government officials soared from 1,200 to 4,000 a year.

Caught in the crossfire were two American military advisors, Major Dale R. Buis and Master Sergeant Chester M. Ovnand, killed with two South Vietnamese guards and an eight-year-old boy in a raid on a camp northeast of Saigon on July 8, 1959. Then a correspondent for *Time*, I duly reported the incident, never imagining that their names would head the list of nearly 60,000 American dead engraved on the Vietnam Memorial in Washington, D.C.

From his seat in the Senate, John F. Kennedy declared that Vietnam was "not only a proving ground for democracy in Asia," but a "test of American responsibility and determination." He felt it vital that the line be held against "the relentless pressure of the Chinese Communists." As president, he accordingly increased aid to Diem, sending him helicopters and providing his army with U.S. advisors, whose ranks grew from 800 in 1961 to 16,000 in 1963. American

Old U.S. shell casings lie beside a road in Quang Tri Province, the site of the demilitarized zone during the "American" war and the scene of some of the heaviest fighting. Leftover ordnance, says American photographer Dick Swanson, who covered the war for Life *magazine, is still a common sight in the region.*
Photo by Dick Swanson, USA

officials were aware of Diem's shortcomings, but deposing him was no easy matter. The U.S. ambassador in Saigon, Henry Cabot Lodge, secretly encouraged Diem's generals, who had been plotting a coup of their own. On the afternoon of November 1, 1963, they made their move. After a day in hiding, Diem and his brother Nhu surrendered—only to be murdered in cold blood.

Three weeks later, Kennedy was assassinated. A few days after being sworn in, Lyndon Johnson asserted that he would not "lose Vietnam," essentially signalling a continuation of his predecessor's policy. Caught in the middle of the 1964 election campaign, however, he was reluctant to initiate any action—until the following August, when the White House received what turned out to be a false report that a South Vietnamese patrol boat, operating in tandem with U.S. forces in the Tonkin Gulf, had been attacked. Anxious to bolster himself against Republican accusations that he was "soft on Communism," Johnson ordered American airplanes to bomb North Vietnam and, at the same time, asked Congress to pass a resolution giving him a free hand in Southeast Asia. Without investigating, the House of Representatives unanimously endorsed his request, which the Senate approved with only two dissenting votes. In fact, no incident had actually occurred, but the bipartisan vote on Capitol Hill, combined with the bombing, silenced his Republican adversary, Barry Goldwater—and contributed to Johnson's landslide at the polls.

It did not change the situation in Vietnam, however. By late 1964, North Vietnamese regulars had moved into the south, as the new leaders of South Vietnam argued among themselves. Johnson waffled, while his staff looked for a chance to spur him into action. It came on February 7, 1965, when the Vietcong stormed a base in Pleiku, in the southern highlands, killing eight U.S. advisors. American planes immediately started bombing North Vietnam, and others soon began operations from a field near the seaside town of Danang. On March 8, Marines in full battle regalia splashed onto the beach to secure the base perimeter. The first U.S. combat troops to land in Vietnam, they were just the thin wedge of an expeditionary force that, by the end of 1967, would number more than half a million.

FLOTSAM FROM THE FRENCH WAR INCLUDES this howitzer at Dien Bien Phu. The decisive May 1954 victory of the Vietminh here is credited to the patience and tactical acumen of General Vo Nguyen Giap, whose troops lugged heavy weapons like this one piece by piece through the jungle to sites high above the French garrison. As Giap's artillery rained mortar on the French positions, his infantry dug several hundred miles of tunnels around the French base, gradually eliminating all possible avenues of retreat. The entire effort required months of labor, but Giap could not afford to lose. He considered victory here essential to strengthen the Vietnamese position at the negotiations in Geneva.

Photo by Dinh Quang Thanh, Vietnam

BOMB CRATERS DOT HA TINH PROVINCE,
an area struck frequently by U.S. bombers
targetting the industrial city of Vinh and the Ho
Chi Minh Trail, the chief supply line of the
Vietcong. All told, the U.S. dropped more than six
million tons of bombs on Vietnam. Many of the
resulting craters are now stocked with fish.
Photo by Tara Sosrowardoyo, Indonesia

A TRAP DOOR OPENS TO THE CU CHI TUNNELS,
an intricate network of narrow underground
passages that once stretched from Ho Chi Minh
City's suburbs to the Cambodian border. Begun
in the 1940s during the war against the French
and extended in the early 1960s, this extraordinary
underground maze once accommodated up to
6,000 soldiers. A Vietcong stronghold in the war
against the Americans, the region around the
tunnel—dubbed the Iron Triangle—was defoliated,
napalmed, and turned into a free-fire zone. In 1969,
B-52 saturation bombing raids finally destroyed
most of the subterranean network, but by then the
tide of the war had turned. Today tourists can visit
the tunnels, which have since been enlarged to
accommodate "wider" Westerners, in the village of
Ben Duoc, 47 miles northwest of Ho Chi Minh City.
Photo by Guglielmo de' Micheli, Italy

A "LOVE" TATTOO AND A DANGLING PEACE
sign evoke an era that this young postcard
salesman can only imagine. He and his friends
peddle souvenirs near Ho Chi Minh City's
Notre Dame Cathedral.
Photo by Sarah Leen, USA˙

IN A JUNKYARD IN THANH TRACH VILLAGE,
Quang Binh Province, Indonesian photographer Tara Sosrowardoyo came across an
extraordinary scene. "A group of children were
gathered around two men who were pounding
at this bomb with enormous steel mallets,"
recalls Sosrowardoyo. "I have absolutely no
experience with bombs, but I took the picture
thinking, if they go, I suppose I go, too." What
the Vietnamese knew, but Sosrowardoyo
didn't, was that the bomb's firing mechanism
had deteriorated. The photographer was right
to worry, however. Hospitals report a steady
flow of farmers and scrap metal searchers who
have been killed or injured by stepping on live
landmines and bombs.
Photo by Tara Sosrowardoyo, Indonesia

HO CHI MINH'S PERSONAL photographer, Dinh Dang Dich, 70, *(top)* spent every day with the founder of the modern Vietnamese state for 23 years, from 1946 until Ho's death in 1969. In the 1940s and early 1950s that often meant shooting and developing pictures under extremely adverse conditions, like using a cave for a darkroom. Ho, Dich says, was sometimes an unwilling subject, but Dich paid him no mind. "I'm a photographer," he says, "so that's what I did—take pictures."
Photo by Robin Moyer, USA

VIETNAM'S GREATEST LIVING military hero, General Vo Nguyen Giap, 83, *(above)* departs a commemoration of the 40th anniversary of the battle of Dien Bien Phu, one of his most well-known military successes. The Vietnamese victory here in 1954 turned the momentum of the war against the French. Giap is also the architect of the strategies for the Tet Offensive and the battle at Khe Sanh, considered to be the turning point in the "American" War.
Photo by Catherine Karnow, USA

THE COMPOSER OF VIETNAM'S national anthem, "Advancing Army Song," Van Cao, 71, has been both reviled and celebrated during his long artistic career. Ho Chi Minh chose his song in 1945, but twelve years later, Cao was ostracized for daring to criticize the party's land redistribution program. Though his anthem could be heard everywhere, his poetry and paintings were banned, and he was forced to earn money composing musical scores for movies. Not until 1987 were he and his music rehabilitated.
Photo by Raphaël Gaillarde, France

The Prime Minister of Vietnam, Vo Van Kiet, 71, has been an advocate of reform for most of his political career. In 1975, after the end of the war, Kiet served as party secretary and mayor of Ho Chi Minh City, where he was entrusted with introducing socialism to the south. But when food and industrial production fell in the late 1970s, he became convinced that more flexible policies were needed to stimulate growth. He rose to the position of Prime Minister in 1991, largely because he was a strong advocate of the liberal policies of *doi moi*, or "renewal," initiated by his predecessors. A few years ago, he was asked about the risks this course had brought him. He replied that one must choose between "producing wealth but violating regulations, or continuing to sustain failures and earning praise."
Photo by P.F. Bentley, USA

En route to a cemetery in the dunes near Nhan Trach, a fishing village in the province of Quang Binh, Nguyen Thi Xuan, 73, *(following page)* takes hold of her grandson's hand. She will light incense over the four graves that belong to her two children and their spouses. Of the four, two died as soldiers. The others were killed in U.S. naval bombardments.
Photo by Vu Quoc Khanh, Vietnam

Vu Quoc Khanh

A HAPLESS RECRUIT FALLS BEHIND HIS
fellow conscripts. Vietnam still drafts young
men at age eighteen, but has cut their time of
service from three years to two. Since 1986,
the Army has been reduced by about 50
percent, to some 600,000 troops. This has
added to unemployment problems,
particularly among urban vets and officers,
who find it difficult to compete for jobs.
Photo by Vu Dat, Vietnam

IN THE HO CHI MINH READING ROOM OF
the 301st Army Regiment, located on the
outskirts of Hanoi, soldiers read the day's news.
Before photographer Rick Smolan arrived at
the base, he was told that no Western photographer had ever been there before. "I'd been
warned that they might not be very cooperative," Smolan says, "But when I showed up in
the reading room, one of the soldiers looked up
from his newspaper, looked at me, then said
my name out loud. Another guy did the same
thing, and before I knew it, the whole room
was chanting my name. It turned out there
was an article about *Passage to Vietnam* on
the front page. All of a sudden I was a celebrity
and given full access to the entire base."
Photo by Rick Smolan, USA

ALREADY A NATIONAL HERO AT THE AGE OF 22,
Lt. Colonel Nguyen Thi Chien, 65, shows off
the 18 medals she has been awarded since she first
took up arms at the age of 16. Chien told American photographer Denise Rocco of the years
she spent fighting the French, the Japanese, and
the Americans; how she taught women's resistance
groups to make their own weapons, dig tunnels,
and steal guns. "Her stories poured out of
her with pride and emotion," says Rocco. "I was
entirely mesmerized by her strength and the
sadness of what she had experienced. Then, all of
a sudden, she said, 'In the words of Ho Chi Minh,
we shall forget the past and greet the future with
open arms.' I could barely fight back the tears."
Photo by Denise Rocco, USA

VIETNAMESE SOLDIERS WAIT TO MARCH
in a parade honoring the 35th anniversary of
Ho Chi Minh's visit to Cat Ba Island.
Photo by Bruno Barbey, France

RETIRED VIETCONG COLONEL DO SA, holds a Vietnamese flag on the sand at China Beach, Danang, near the site where the first American combat troops splashed ashore in 1965. Photographer Dirck Halstead was the UPI photographer assigned to cover the Marines' landing 29 years ago. He recalls that the welcoming committee then included a few local officials and twenty girls in traditional *ao dais*. On his recent visit, Halstead, now a *Time* photographer, thought it be would be great to find one of them. Or better yet, somebody who had fought against the Marines.

When he got there, he says, "They took me to a house in downtown Danang to meet a very distinguished looking man. His name was Do Sa, and he had been in command of Regiment 70, the Vietcong corps that went up against the Marines in

that very first battle, at a place called Chu Lai, in August of 1965. His job had been to test the Marines in battle. He was a very honored veteran. I wanted to get him back to China Beach, where he'd been the real 'welcoming' committee."

Do Sa agreed, and on the day of the photograph, he showed up "wearing a plain old jacket like mine," says Halstead. "But he opened up a bag he had brought with him, put on about 30 medals and epaulettes, and all of a sudden, he was a colonel again. I photographed him in this gorgeous light, standing erect and holding a Vietnamese flag. I thought, that's the picture of a winning colonel. It's a very important picture for me."
Photo by Dirck Halstead, USA

A VETERAN OF BOTH THE FRENCH AND the American wars, Le Chau Phong, 71, *(right),* today tends the graves at a cemetery in Thanh Trach village, Quang Binh Province. Says Indonesian photographer Tara Sosrowardoyo, "I asked Phong if he knew anyone who had been buried here, and he said, 'Yes. Many of my friends are in this cemetery.' He sat down on the grave site of one of his friends who had died quite young, and started talking about him; about how so many people had died in the war and how ridiculous and what a waste it all was and then he just started to sob. Without thinking about it, I found myself sitting there crying, too. I felt kind of embarrassed in front of my interpreter, and looked up, only to see tears on his face also."
Photo by Tara Sosrowardoyo, Indonesia

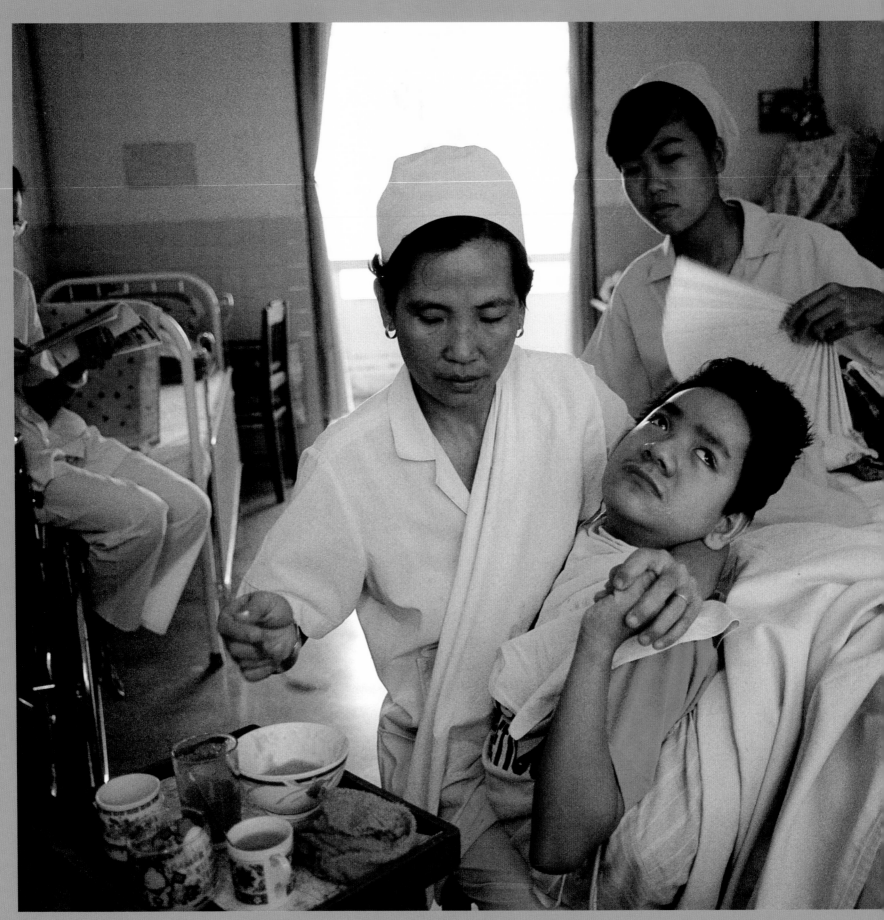

Separated from his Siamese twin, a patient is fed at the Tu Du Maternity Hospital in Ho Chi Minh City.

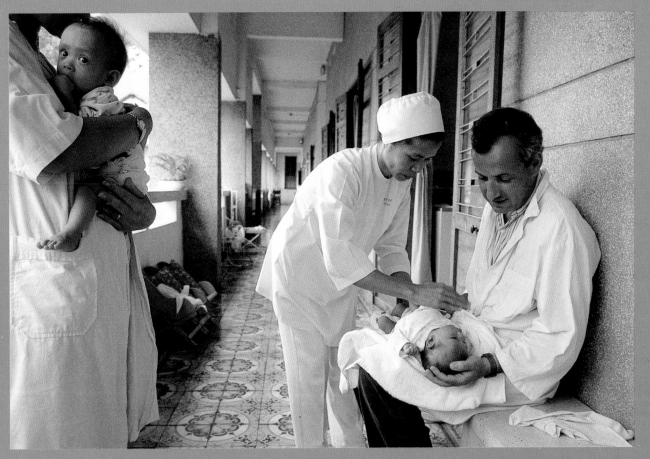

In addition to its work with victims of Agent Orange, Tu Du helps place orphans with families in Vietnam and abroad.

THE NEVER-ENDING WAR

Photos by Lise Sarfati

The Tu Du Maternity Hospital in Ho Chi Minh City has taken charge of one of the grimmest legacies of the "American" war. The hospital maintains a special room, open to the public, in which it has preserved the bodies of deformed fetuses. These babies, the hospitals' administration says, were born to women exposed to Agent Orange, the herbicide used by the U.S. to defoliate the forests of Vietnam.

Not all of the babies born at Tu Du are de-formed. The hospital delivers hundreds of healthy babies every week. But it is the jars and the wards on the second floor, where deformed children who survive birthing are cared for, that attract the most attention.

Altogether, the U.S. dumped eleven million gallons of Agent Orange on Vietnam. America has yet to acknowledge that its defoliation campaigns caused the health problems. For the Vietnamese, there is ample evidence. Liver cancer is widespread in the generation which breathed the poison. And among their descendants, malformed limbs and cleft palates are common. One other statistical anomaly involves Siamese twins. A nation Vietnam's size could normally expect one such birth every ten or fifteen years. Instead, it has been seeing ten pairs per year.

NGUYEN THI THI FINDS SOLACE in the shell of the La Vang Catholic Church in Quang Tri Province. The cathedral was destroyed in 1972, during the American summer offensive, around the same time that Thi's husband and son were killed in fighting near the city of Danang. For the six million Catholics of Vietnam, the La Vang Cathedral is a place of tremendous spiritual resonance. An apparition of the Virgin Mary is said to have appeared at a small church on this site in 1798, and for many years, the anniversary date of that sighting attracted up to 300,000 Vietnamese pilgrims. In the years after the war, Hanoi kept a tight rein on the Catholic Church, and visits to La Vang decreased. But a renewal of interest in religion among young people and a willingness on Hanoi's part to tolerate independent religious observance have brought more worshippers. In 1993, nearly 25,000 people came to La Vang on the day of the anniversary.
Photo by Dick Swanson, USA

THREE

PORTRAIT OF CHANGE

BY PETER SAIDEL

T HE MOMENT THE RAIN TAPERS OFF IN HO CHI MINH CITY, adolescent street hawkers re-emerge from beneath the awnings to continue their endless search for new customers. Ten year olds selling lottery tickets run from food stalls to tailor shops, looking for people who believe that today might be their lucky day. Then commuters peer out from under the eaves, wipe pools of water from their new Honda motorbikes, and roar off into the sprawling arms of the metropolis.

One Hanoian friend living in Ho Chi Minh City complains, "This city has no soul." But natives turn defensive at the suggestion that they have no depth. They may seem preoccupied with commerce and fashion, but they also have romance and sentimentality, and, at their heart, they have Saigon.

Ho Chi Minh City includes a dozen thriving commercial districts with different names, and at the center is Saigon—District One—with its old French villas, wide open streets, and an avenue of boutiques running from the Notre Dame Cathedral to the river. Ho Chi Minh City is a vibrant, exciting economic tiger. But everyone still calls the city Saigon and, as everyone knows, Saigon is not only a place for commerce, but for experience.

Ho Chi Minh City is young and hopeful and on the move. It has been almost a decade since Hanoi introduced *doi moi,* a collection of reforms and new attitudes that essentially released Vietnam from the doctrinaire approach to socialism which Ho Chi Minh's contemporaries had pursued since the revolu-

Power and phone lines criss-cross farmland outside Quang Xuan, in Ha Tinh Province. Although Soviet-built hydroelectric plants have brought more electricity to some areas, rural electrification projects have a long way to go. Photo by Tara Sosrowardoyo, Indonesia

tionary leader's death in 1969. Meaning renewal, *doi moi* opened Vietnamese society in unprecedented ways, by allowing foreign investment and greater freedoms of expression and worship. It has permitted the Vietnamese to own and operate their own businesses and, perhaps most importantly, earn money for themselves.

It is this new opportunity that infuses the air in Ho Chi Minh City. Not that the Vietnamese actually needed any encouragement. The entrepreneurial spirit seems almost second nature to most of them. It's just that before *doi moi*, they had to pursue money-making behind closed doors, under the dark cloud of the black market. Now it's all legal, and the rush to get to the marketplace is furious. It is not uncommon to see men and women holding down two or three jobs, or working on construction sites long past midnight, their efforts illuminated by only a few bare bulbs and the blue spark of a welder's gun.

But *doi moi* is not only about making money. It is about enjoying it, by seeing what the world has to offer, by testing the limits of change. Now that the country has opened its doors, a period of experimentation has begun, especially among those who are under 21, which, by a recent count, is almost half the country.

On Teacher's Day (a national favorite), on Reunification Day, on Christmas, and to a lesser extent, every Sunday night, the downtown streets of Ho Chi Minh City are packed with young people having fun.

They deck themselves out in glitter duds, striking poses while moving at 25 m.p.h. on their 70cc Honda motorbikes. Boys with James Dean hairdos and dangling cigarettes loosen their shoulders to whip like snakes through traffic. The girls ride behind, chatting, sometimes sidesaddle and at ease, poised cross-legged, as if at a debutante ball.

True, Vietnam is an ancient country, with thousands of years of tradition behind it. But in Ho Chi Minh City, and increasingly in Hanoi, the old blends

Rush hour on Hanoi's Kham Thien Street. The workday for most Vietnamese begins at the crack of dawn. An hour after sunrise, most city streets are clogged with traffic. Photo by Joe McNally, USA

125

with the new in surprising ways. I asked a friend once if he liked the *ao dai*, the Vietnamese woman's traditional dress. Though noticeably transparent, the white *ao dai* has somehow become the high school uniform in Ho Chi Minh City.

"Of course I like *ao dai*," he said. "I am Vietnamese!"

"And why do Vietnamese like the *ao dai*?" I asked.

"The *ao dai*," he said, "is part mystery, part revelation."

Indeed, it seems as though tradition is unable to hold young Vietnamese down. As Indo-chic struts down fashion show runways in Paris, the youth of Ho Chi Minh City are trying out the rudiments of MTV vogue, albeit slightly outdated, and learning to dress like Madonna and Stevie Nicks or Sid Vicious and Don Johnson all at once.

The cruising teenagers seem unconcerned that, for their parents, the air is cluttered with ghosts. The youth can barely remember the war. How could they be bothered by it? Their parents, though, begin every other sentence with "Before 1975…" and end it with nostalgia: for their own youth, for excitement, even for the old French names of the tree-lined boulevards.

Like them, I'm too young to remember the war. But one evening I stopped in front of the famous Rex Hotel, one of the city's many stage sets "before 1975," and a teenage girl stepped up to me, and said in perfect bar-girl English: "Hey you! Long time no see! Remember me? Long time no see!" Yes, it has been a long time, I felt like telling her, but how could I forget?

Saigon was always a market for the commodities of pleasure. Although today's Ho Chi Minh City is too busy to look back, it isn't too busy to have fun. Everywhere are garden cafés with dark hideaways, and discos where swanky singers in miniskirts croon slow-dance ballads under dreamy blue neon, and "taxi-dancers" wait for single men as they have been waiting for twenty years.

The people of the city live in a generous world. They have an expression,

Only seventeen of Hanoi's 496 intersections have traffic lights, most of them installed in the last five years. Policemen stationed at these busy corners enforce traffic laws and switch the lights from red to green. Photo by Raphaël Gaillarde, France

"Five won, five lost." It means: Relax, take a chance. You may lose but you'll always win again.

Their attitude is different than in the north. Northerners use each word with caution, and they speak with jabbing, dramatic tones that make every word punch with meaning; southerners are more easy to gamble, and their voices slip and drawl.

Northerners trust only in sturdy tradition: this is what has helped them survive so far. Southerners, on the other hand, are more inclined to place their faith with all religions—just to cover the bases. On Christmas, crowds of people, regardless of religion, stand outside the churches just to be close to the action; on the new lunar month, teenagers don't only crowd into Buddhist temples, they also may stop into one of the city's several Hindu shrines, just to be on the safe side.

On the outskirts of the city, there is a shrine called Giac Lam Pagoda. It is a quiet, wooden temple, filled with relics aged by incense, lit with a smoky light that angles through a slatted roof onto a black-and-white tile floor.

When I was last there, I watched a crew from a Saigon film studio. The place was as bright as a stage set, as actors dressed like Vietnamese emperors stood around smoking cigarettes and waiting to film the next scene. To some foreign visitors, the actors seemed disrespectful; but the people of Ho Chi Minh City know that there is a time to stop and pray and attend to affairs of the soul, and a time to make business. And now, they know, it's time to get back on the motorcycle and ride.

Outside the Ma Long shipyard in Quang Ninh Province, a poster warns, "Labor Safety Regulation is the Law." A hard-hatted worker arrives for his shift. Photo by Barry Lewis, United Kingdom

CENTRAL HANOI'S HOAN KIEM LAKE IS A
popular site for early morning exercise. A
visitor strolling around the lake at dawn will
encounter old women playing badminton,
teenage joggers, and a few pedestrians
searching for turtles. Legend has it that a magic
turtle once rose from the depths of the lake to
retrieve a sword, which the Emperor Le Loi
used to drive out the Chinese. Thus the lake's
name Ho Hoan Kiem means "Lake of the
Restored Sword." Recent municipal conserva-
tion efforts have centered on cleaning up the
tiny body of water, which Hanoians consider
the jewel of the city. One result of the efforts
has been increased sightings of turtles.
Photo by P.F. Bentley, USA

IT'S 8 A.M., LONG PAST WAKE-UP FOR MOST
Vietnamese, but this group sleeps late. They've set up their army cot on the divider of one of Ho Chi Minh City's wide boulevards.
Photo by Paul Chesley, USA

A Japanese refrigerator, its label a
thing to flaunt, is among the material
rewards earned by this two-income couple.
Dr. Nguyen Thi Hoang, 42, is a pathologist
at Thai Nguyen Hospital in Bac Thai Province.
Her husband, Tran Phuc Hoi, is an engineer
and director of a local steel mill. Also at
the table are their children Anh Tho, 17, Phuc
Ngoc, 11, and Dr. Hoang's father.
Photo by Pedro Coll, Spain

JUST BACK FROM THE MATERNITY WARD in Ho Chi Minh City, three-day-old Nguyen Quang Cuong feeds off his mother's milk, while his father, Nguyen Van Mai, 26, checks out the bottled variety.

Photo by Lise Sarfati, France

AFTER FOURTEEN YEARS IN CALIFORNIA, Phuong Anh Nguyen has returned home. Before her thirteenth birthday, she and her family had tried and failed to escape Vietnam many times, surviving pirates, shipwrecks, and a half dozen other misfortunes. Finally, in 1978, they made it to the U.S., where they settled in Pasadena. Phuong graduated from San Jose State College and first returned to Vietnam in 1990 with a medical relief group. One year later, she moved to Ho Chi Minh City, where she now designs interiors for bars and restaurants, including Q-bar, which she also helps run. One of the city's hot spots, the name is a pun on *Viet Kieu*, which means "overseas Vietnamese." There are some two million Vietnamese now living outside of Vietnam. Approximately half of them are in the U.S. Riding behind Phuong on her restored Lambretta motor scooter is Nguyen Troung Luu Thuy, a local clothes designer.
Photo by Catherine Karnow, USA

Familiar labels appear at a mom-and-
daughter food store in Hanoi. Many such goods
are smuggled from China, Cambodia, or
Thailand and may well be the real thing. Other
products are outright fakes.
Photo by Joe McNally, USA

Peter Turnley, USA

Robin Moyer, USA

Jay Dickman, USA

Peter Turnley, USA

Radhika Chalasani, USA

Monica Almeida, USA

Barry Lewis, United Kingdom

On a typical Vietnamese street, automobiles are the exception, rather than the norm, their numbers greatly overwhelmed by bicycles and motorbikes, and a never-ending stream of wheeled miscellany. Indeed, the clever uses to which the simple wheel has been put is a stunning tribute to the nation's drive and ingenuity. The common cyclo, or pedicab, is frequently asked to perform the functions of a schoolbus, semi, or minivan, while hybrid vehicles, like the three-wheeled minitruck and the flatbed motorcycle are popular configurations. Of course, when engine power is too expensive, broken down, or simply unavailable, there is always plain, old-fashioned elbow grease.

WEARING A TRADITIONAL *AO DAI,* ONE
corner held up to keep it clear of the oily chain,
a young cyclist lends a touch of elegance to
Ho Chi Minh City traffic. An import from
China in the mid-18th century, the *ao dai*
became virtually mandatory during the
reign of Emperor Minh Mang, who imposed
the wearing of trousers on the entire female
population. In the 1930s, the outfit was
modernized with the creation of a greater
variety of colors and designs, innovations
which have evolved into today's styles. The
color white is worn by secondary school girls.
Photo by Peter Turnley, USA

A WEDDING DRESS—AVAILABLE FOR SALE
or rent—mesmerizes a passerby on a street in
downtown Hanoi. Until recently, many mar-
riages in Vietnam were arranged by the parents
of the bride and groom. Today, however, most
Vietnamese choose their own spouses, though
many couples postpone nuptials, in part,
because the government is encouraging them
to have no more than two children. Under
the limit, they feel less pressure to rush to start
families. Even so, women who wait until their
30s may be considered *e,* or "little in demand."
Photo by Nicole Bengiveno, USA

THE HEIGHT OF TODAY'S FASHION, POLKA DOTS
proliferate on a wet street in the city of Hue. As the
Vietnamese economy opens up, consumers enjoy a
wider selection of products, but they do not yet have
the varied selection of styles that Western shoppers
take for granted.
Photo by Diego Goldberg, Argentina

IN ADDITION TO TEN-CENT HAIRCUTS, OUT-
door barbers along Hanoi's Quang Trung Street
will also take a little off the forehead, ears,
and neck. At the end of the day, they will take
down their mirrors and shelves, hung on
the wall of a hospital compound, and pack
away their chairs and equipment. Clumps
of trimmed hair on the sidewalk are the only
sign that they've been here.
Photo by Nicole Bengiveno, USA

FLARING NATURAL GAS
burnoffs light up the White
Tiger oil fields, some 75
miles offshore of Vung Tau.
In 1994, Vietsovpetro, a
Russian-Vietnamese joint
venture, drew some 40
million barrels from White
Tiger, all of it taken to other
countries for refining.
Vietnam lacks the pipelines
and refineries that would
enable it to take full
advantage of its enormous
gas and oil reserves,
estimated by one study to lie
between 1.5 to 3 billion
barrels, equivalent to those
of oil-rich Brunei.
Photo by Andy Levin, USA

UNDER THE EYE OF VIETNAM'S most famous cyclist, workers turn out bicycles at the French-built Vitta Factory in Hanoi. Sales of domestic bikes country-wide have been hurt in recent years by better-quality models smuggled in from China, and, of course, the growing appetite for motorbikes. Strong markets for Vietnam's output in Cuba, Bulgaria, and Laos, however, help keep production at about 100,000 bikes a year. Prices range from $35 for the top-of-the-line *Doan The* ("Corporate"), to $20 for the *Huu Nghi* ("Friendship").
Photo by Robin Moyer, USA

A brick mason in Vinh, Nghe An Province, eyeballs his work. The Vietnamese lack the facilities to manufacture sophisticated tools, but they are ingenious at improvisation.
Photo by Tara Sosrowardoyo, Indonesia

Wet gravel, mixed with sand, makes its way to the roof of the future Post Office Guest House in Dong Hoi, Quang Binh Province. In both public buildings and private homes, Vietnamese are using architecture to express a sense of whimsy and joy long repressed by years of war and economic hardship.
Photo by Vu Quoc Khanh, Vietnam

The Miracle of Silk

Photos by Stephanie Maze

Used to make parachutes, cold cream, surgical sutures, tennis-racket strings, bicycle tires, and, of course, fabric, silk is one of the most versatile substances known to man. It was more than 4,000 years ago that the Chinese first discovered its miraculous qualities. For more than two millennia, they kept the method of its manufacture a secret, threatening anyone who broke the silence with death by torture. Ultimately, of course, the secret leaked out. According to one legend, the Byzantine Emperor Justinian brought silk-making to the West by sending monks to China as spies. It is said that they returned to Constantinople with mulberry leaves—the only food that the best silkworms will eat—and a few eggs, which they hid in hollow canes.

The insect whose cocoon fiber is used to make silk is a species of caterpillar, known to silkmakers and scientists as *bombyx mori*. Endowed with an extraordinary appetite, it typically increases its body weight 10,000 times in the span of its 25- to 28-day life. After shedding its skin four times, it builds a cocoon by ejecting a wet protein that instantly hardens into fiber. Produced at the rate of about a foot a minute, this fiber extends nearly one mile and is stronger than a comparable filament of steel. Without the

Stacked trays of cocoons are sorted by size, color, and density.

interruption of the silkmaker, the pupa inside the cocoon would ultimately emerge as a egg-laying moth, destroying the cocoon in the process. But if the pupa is killed midway through the cycle, the cocoon can be preserved, and its filament unwound to make silk.

American photographer Stephanie Maze visited Vietnam's biggest silk factory, the Union of Sericulture Enterprises, or Viseri, outside the town of Bao Loc in Lam Dong Province.

Viseri employees pull the strands away from the cocoons and feed them into the machines that twist them into thread and wind them onto spools.

Cocoons are boiled to kill the worm inside and loosen the strands.

Skeins of new silk are ready for dying.

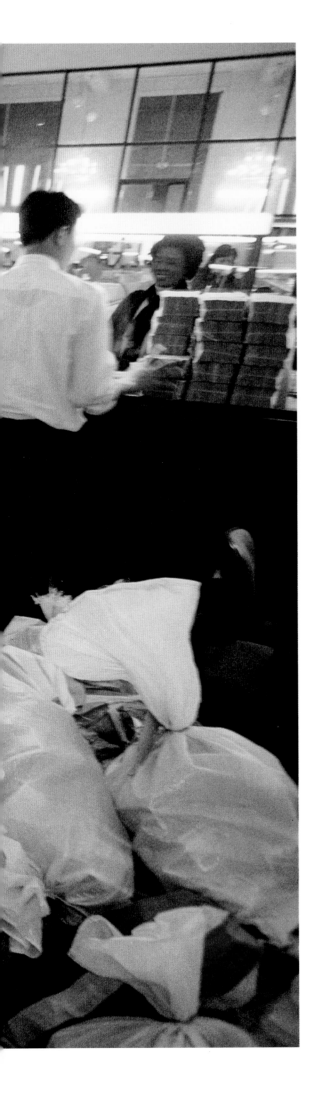

A TEXTILE COMPANY EXECUTIVE PLACES A call before setting off in his 1930 Citroën. The free-market economy holds great rewards for those with college educations, a second language, family ties, and, perhaps most important, entrepreneurial hustle.
Photo by Peter Turnley, USA

A DAY'S WORTH OF CASH ARRIVES ON THE main floor of the State Bank in Hanoi. Consumers are accustomed to carrying enormous bundles of Vietnamese dong in their pockets, the result of the government's inability to pay its own bills. By the late 1980s, annual inflation had risen to almost 500 percent. Since 1992, the government has spent its money more wisely, reducing that rate to about five percent.
Photo by Robin Moyer, USA

A TRAY OF VIETNAMESE SPECIALTIES—
steamed crab, meat-shrimp dumplings, meat-stuffed tomatoes, and pork roll, to name a few—heads to the upstairs dining room of Hanoi's Viet Huong Restaurant. Indoor restaurants, most of them in people's homes, are proliferating in Hanoi, which had a scant half dozen in the late 1980s. Most are family run—four generations operate the Viet Huong—and prices are inexpensive by Western standards. A typical four-course meal for one costs approximately US$2.50.
Photo by Lois Raimondo, USA

ALTHOUGH THEY ARE ENTITLED TO A 60-
minute lunch break, workers at the Haiphong Seafood Factory prefer to eat fast, and use most of their break time for a nap.
Photo by P.F. Bentley, USA

THIS MANICURED YOUNG LADY APPEARS TO have it made. Her mother's wheels are a Honda Dream Two—as good as two-wheelers get in Vietnam. The veil is not just for fashion. It helps protect the eyes from Hanoi's dust.
Photo by Raphaël Gaillarde, France

IN AN ALLEY IN CHOLON, A YOUNGSTER gets an early afternoon meal. Hot days find many people out on the streets, hoping to catch a cool breeze and a whiff of gossip from their neighbors.
Photo by Radhika Chalasani, USA

CHILDREN PLAY AT HUE'S IMPERIAL PALACE,
(previous page) where the Nguyen dynasty held
court from 1802 until 1945.
Photo by Monica Almeida, USA

THE HANOI SCHOOL OF MUSIC'S CURRICULUM
includes Western and Vietnamese traditional music,
as well as theory and dance. The 500 students are
selected through a national competition. These two
work on an afternoon assignment after a morning
at elementary school; older students take a full load
of academic classes on top of music instruction.
Photo by Joe McNally, USA

Western ABCs set Vietnam apart from the rest of continental Asia. The Roman alphabet came to Vietnam primarily via Alexandre de Rhodes, a 17th-century French Jesuit. On his arrival, Rhodes contemptuously likened the country's tonal language—then written in Chinese-based ideographs—to "twittering birds." Yet six months later, he was preaching in Vietnamese. And in order to spread the Gospel, he perfected *quoc ngu*, as this script is called, using accents to indicate which of the language's six tones the words required. This written form of colloquial Vietnamese shattered the monopoly of scholarship once held by the mandarins of the emperor's court, opening up a new form of communication among the emerging middle class, the intelligentsia, peasants, and, not least, future revolutionaries.
Photo by Randy Olson, USA

VIETNAM BOASTS AN 88% LITERACY RATE,
which is exceptionally high for a country with
such a large amount of poverty. The Vietnamese
hope that their exceedingly well-educated
population will attract foreign investment.
"An ignorant nation is a weak nation," Ho Chi
Minh said. "Illiteracy is an enemy as dangerous
as invasion and famine." At the Quang Phu
Cau school in Ha Tay Province, thirteen-year-old
Nguyen Thi Hoa listens to a lecture.
Photo by Patrick Tehan, USA

TEACHER VU KIM HANH CLAPS THE METER
to the song "Spring Calls," as Vu Dien Thao,
thirteen, a student at Hanoi's Music School,
struggles with the *dan ty ba.* This four-
stringed, fretted lute, similar to China's *pi pa,*
is used in both Vietnam's traditional music
and in a new style of music, developed in the
last 50 years, which draws heavily on Western
rhythms and scales.
Photo by Joe McNally, USA

AT AN ATELIER IN HANOI'S OLD QUARTER, an artist copies an old photograph. Business at this studio remains brisk, due in large part to the scarcity of photographic equipment and supplies. Customers interested in a modernized reproduction can request color versions, either in gouache or oil. The cost for this monochrome rendering: approximately US$1.
Photo by Raphaël Gaillarde, France

HANOI'S FINE ART SCHOOL, FOUNDED BY THE French in 1925, enjoys renewed political freedom. Its 100 students are no longer confined to the narrow messages of socialist propaganda. At the same time, though, few Vietnamese artists, whether in the school or outside it, employ explicit political themes in their work, preferring instead to concentrate on more aesthetic challenges. The buckets to the right of the model are charcoal heaters intended to keep her goosebumps at bay.
Photo by Raphaël Gaillarde, France

In order to shoot the performers of Hanoi's Big Top, American photographer Mary Ellen Mark chose to work with a 4 x 5 view camera, which she felt would give the photographs an additional depth and clarity. Still, the lights and set-up time that the camera requires introduced a little chaos to her effort. A monkey pedalling a toy car took a dislike to her assistant and charged him, trying to run him down. And an elephant, impatient at having to wait for its portrait to be taken, suddenly took off with its handler in the crook of its trunk. Of all the animals, she says, only the dogs were fully cooperative.

Photos by Mary Ellen Mark, USA

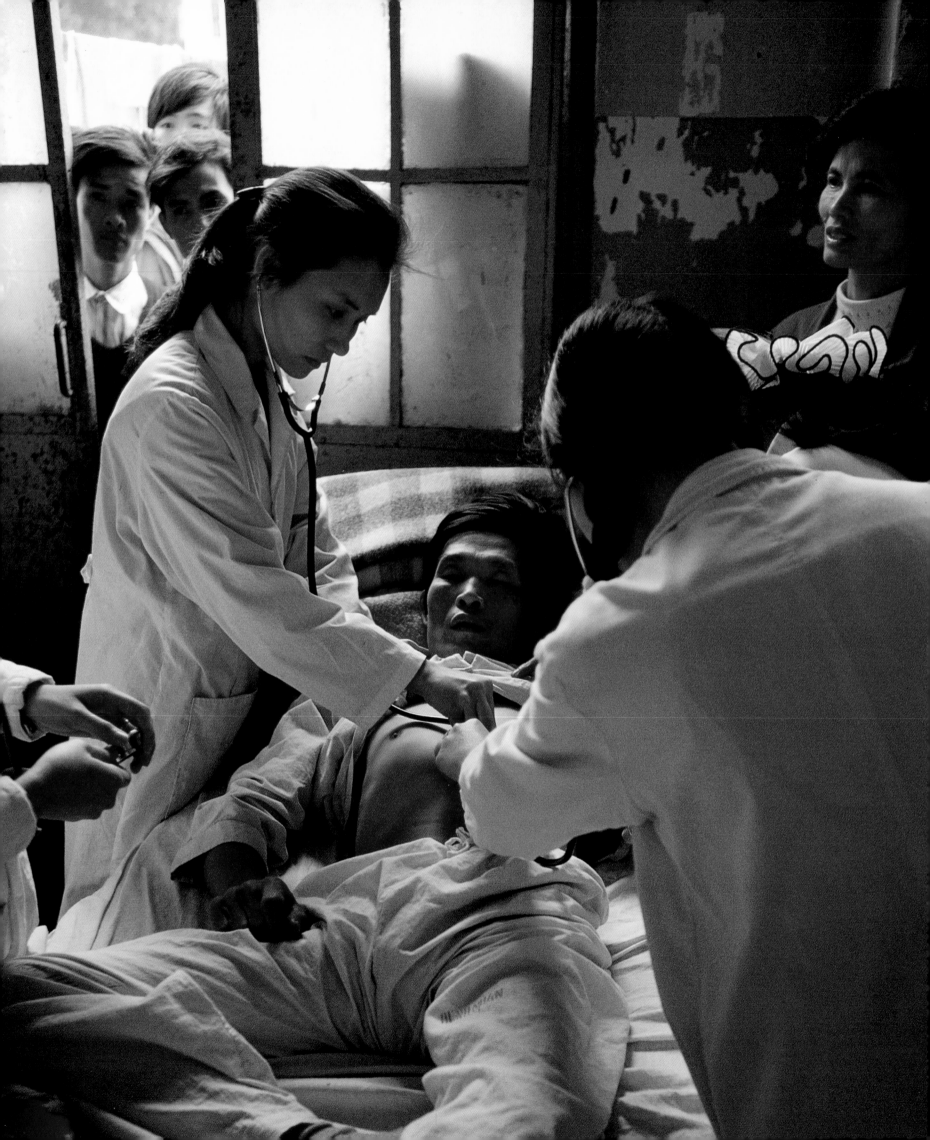

At the Tu Du Maternity Hospital
in Ho Chi Minh City, Dang Thi Hue, 24,
waits for the registrar to issue a birth
certificate. Her son, Nguyen Quang Cuong,
was born at the hospital three days earlier.
Photo by Lise Sarfati, France

Doctors make their rounds of the
cardiology ward at Hanoi's Bach Mai Hospital.
Most foreign medical experts give Vietnam high
marks for its public health system, which
includes some 9,000 clinics around the country
and more than 23,000 doctors, almost twice the
average for developing nations of the same size.
Photo by Peter Steinhauer, USA

BEACH LOVERS MEET THE EARLY TURNING
tide *(previous page)* at Vung Tau, a resort 80
miles southeast of Ho Chi Minh City.
Photo by Andy Levin, USA

IMAGES OF PARADISE HELP A YOUNG WAITER
relax in the lobby of a Ho Chi Minh City restaurant.
Photo by Mark S. Wexler, USA

RUSSIANS TAKE IN THE AFTERNOON AIR AT the seaside resort of Vung Tau. The husbands of these women work for Vietsovpetro, a joint venture between Russia and Vietnam, which operates oil wells offshore. During the late 1970s and early 1980s, when Hanoi and Moscow were more closely aligned, Russians could be found in most major cities, leading many Vietnamese to refer to all Caucasians as *Lien Xo*—literally, "Soviet Union." This inability to distinguish between non-Asian nationalities often had ironic consequences. In Vietnamese films about the "American" war, for example, the roles of American soldiers were frequently played by Russians.
Photo by Andy Levin, USA

SOON AFTER A WHIRLWIND COURTSHIP,
Kim-Huy John Franknedy, a resident
of Marina, California, weds Nguyen Thi
Phuong Phung at a ceremony in her native
Dalat. The couple met in late 1993, after
Franknedy's aunt showed him Phung's
photograph. Intrigued, he wrote a letter,
then arranged a visit. Upon his return to
the U.S., more letters were exchanged.
A few visits later, Franknedy asked Phung
to be his wife. After the wedding,
Phung joined her husband in the U.S.
Photos by Mark S. Wexler, USA

A HANOI BRIDE PICKS HER WAY ALONG a flooded alley near her home with the help of an inventive family member. The groom steadies her from behind, while the rest of the wedding party, some carrying gifts in traditional wedding boxes, find their own way.

Such processions are the essence of a Vietnamese wedding. The celebration begins as the groom and his family go to the bride's house, where he pays respects to her parents and her ancestors. Amidst deafening firecrackers, the couple then walks to the groom's house, where they make offerings to the groom's ancestors

and pay respects to his parents and grandparents. The wedding ceremony itself consists of the reading of a wedding eulogy as well as the sharing of a cup of tea and a betel nut, symbolizing that the couple is now one.

Photo by Bruno Barbey, France

BRIDE NGUYEN LAM BINH, 22, POSES FOR a photograph on what will be her wedding-night bed, in conformance with contemporary Vietnamese custom. A dressmaker, Binh married a 27-year-old clothing salesman in the provincial capital of Ninh Binh. As a not-so-subtle form of encouragement for the newlyweds, some families hang a portrait of a baby boy on the wall over the bed.
Photo by Elliott Erwitt, USA

THE SPORTSMAN'S BODY BUILDING SHOP
offers person-powered treadmills to Danang
residents. Members are inspired by posters of
Arnold Schwarzenegger which have been tacked
to the walls of the humbly equipped gym.
Photo by Dirck Halstead, USA

IN HOI AN, A FISHING COMMUNITY
near Danang, a gunny-sack race is part of
a day-long festival celebrating Ho Chi
Minh's foundation of the Communist Youth
Union in 1931. The participants, some
wearing the red bandanas that identify
them as Pioneers, will also play tug of war
and compete in cooking contests, a way to
teach them survival skills.
Photo by Don Doll, S.J., USA

ON NATIONAL SPORTS DAY, AN EXHAUSTED
student from the Hanoi Institute of Economics
is supported by a friend after finishing the
21st Annual Hanoi Newspaper Road Race.
The participants are high school and university
students from all over Hanoi.
Photo by Nguyen Dan, Vietnam

TWO WOMEN'S SOCCER TEAMS FACE OFF IN
a national tournament in Hong Gai. The
athletes in the yellow jerseys are from Hanoi's
Sports and Physical Culture College.
Their opponents, also from Hanoi, attend
the Technical College.
Photo by Gerald Gay, Australia

Two dragon boats vie for the lead at a competition in Danang, held in honor of the nineteenth anniversary of the city's liberation by the communists. Dragon boat crews, numbering some 40 members, come from cities all over Vietnam to participate in the races. Similar boats have been used in ceremonies in the waters of Southeast Asia for more than 2,000 years.

Photo by Dirck Halstead, USA

On National Sports Day, the Haiphong City Council plays host to the National Wrestling Championships. The Council urges competitors toward "Honest Competition, Unity, and High Achievement."
Photo by P.F. Bentley, USA

During a break in training, the dragon boat crew of Cat Ba Island pauses for a group portrait.
Photo by Yann Arthus-Bertrand, France

A Day at the Races

Photos by Paul Chesley

Ho Chi Minh City's Phu Tho race track opened in 1932 and flourished until the mid-1970s, when the U.S.-backed South Vietnamese government began to crumble. The track's owners, calculating that the odds of their surviving the end of the war were slight, decided to close it down. The new government left the track shuttered, as part of its crackdown on gambling.

Phu Tho got a second chance, however, in 1989, when Philip Chau, a Vietnamese-Chinese businessman, proposed to local government officials that it be reopened. The People's Committee would be partners in the venture

and collect taxes on the track's earnings. Chau put up $200,000, and quickly got the track up and running. Alas for him, the course was so successful that before long his partner seized the whole operation.

Chau plans to open another track soon. Meanwhile, the crowds flock to the meets at Phu Tho. On a good day, 10,000 horse fanciers show up to place their bets. The minimum wager is ten cents, the maximum is US$2. To win, a wagerer must select both the first and second place horse.

FRIENDS FROM DIFFERENT VILLAGES IN
the northernmost reaches of Ha Giang
Province live so far apart that they only see
each other on Sundays, which is market day in
Quan Ban, the district center. These two
Hmong Tay Nung girls take their younger
siblings with them to town. Like most
Vietnamese children, they share responsibility
for child care with their parents and older
brothers and sisters.
Photo by Van Bao, Vietnam

THREE BOYS PADDLE A DRAGON
across Hanoi's Thien Quang Lake.
Photo by Nicole Bengiveno, USA

CATCHING THE BREEZE FROM HIGH ATOP
an abandoned bridge *(previous page)* near the
city of Tra Vinh, in Tra Vinh Province.
Photo by Dilip Mehta, Canada

A SUDDEN CLOUDBURST IN RACH GIA,
a coastal city in Kien Giang Province, sends two
young women scampering for shelter.
Photo by Basil Pao, Hong Kong

PROTECTED FROM THE RAIN BY A PLASTIC bag, perched on a bike seat, a child accompanies her mother on an errand. Though the back of a bicycle may seem a precarious place to seat an infant, Hanoi cyclists are extraordinarily adept at negotiating their way through city traffic. Cars are still relatively rare, while motorcyclists and other cyclists have learned to move through city intersections like fishes in schools, gracefully flowing where the current carries them. Unfortunately, because of increasing motorbike traffic, accidents are on the rise.

Photo by Joe McNally, USA

AT A BODY BUILDER'S CLUB IN HO CHI MINH
City, Tran Chanh Thanh, 22, and friends strut
for French photographer Lise Sarfati. Health
facilities offering weight lifting, aerobics, and
the like are rapidly growing in popularity.
Photo by Lise Sarfati, France

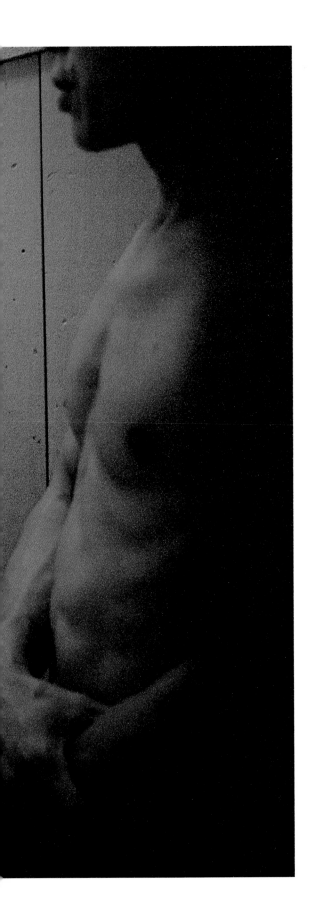

AFTERNOON HEAT IN VUNG TAU CAN GET
rather oppressive. Two boys take a cooling dip
in a water-slide pool.
Photo by Andy Levin, USA

THE BICH CAFE, OVERLOOKING HANOI'S
Hoan Kiem Lake, is a popular hangout for
the 34,000 university students attending
the city's 27 colleges and universities. This
group includes those studying law, art,
architecture—and traffic. The specialty of
the house, *ca phe trung*, is coffee topped
with a mixture of egg and sugar.
Photo by Peter Steinhauer, USA

A DORM AT HANOI UNIVERSITY. FOUNDED in 1956, the school is Vietnam's most prestigious. Shortage of bed space forces students to share. This bunk accommodates four.
Photo by Nicole Bengiveno, USA

AT A PUBLIC HOUSING PROJECT IN Ho Chi Minh City, tenants must pay the government ten percent of their salaries as rent. Housing is scarce, and apartments like these are passed from one family member to the next, or slipped to a friend, for a small fee.
Photo by Paul Chesley, USA

"Tetris," "Othello" and "Joust" are
but a few of the games that can be played at this
video parlor in Hanoi. Opened four years
ago, the place occupies what used to be the front
parlor of proprietor Tran Thy Lich's home.
One thousand dong, equivalent to approximately
ten U.S. cents, buys one hour of play.
Photo by Nicole Bengiveno, USA

March temperatures in Ho Chi Minh
City reach into the mid-90s, while humidity
averages 80 percent. Since air conditioning
is a luxury that few can afford, sleeping on the
street becomes a relatively appealing option.
A mosquito net provides all the shelter this
couple needs.
Photo by Lise Sarfati, France

A balancing act in the surf at Vung Tau
(previous page) reminded American photographer
Andy Levin of the beach back at Coney Island.
Photo by Andy Levin, USA

PUPPETEERS TAKE A BOW AT THE END of an evening's performance by Hanoi's Water Puppet Theater. During the show, these choreographers stand waist-deep in water behind the pagoda set, invisible to the audience, manipulating puppet heroes and heroines with bamboo poles. Remarkably lifelike, the puppets swim, dance, and chase each other across the water's surface. Beside the stage, singers and traditional musicians provide the story lines. The plots of the various sketches are often farcical, which would have delighted Ho Chi Minh. In 1956, he made this centuries-old art an official national treasure by founding the company. "His goal was to bring a smile to the face of children," says Dang Anh Nga, the theater's deputy director.
Photo by Bruno Barbey, France

AN ACTRESS CHECKS HER MAKEUP IN A mirror backstage before a performance of the *Cai Luong,* or "renovated theater" in Ho Chi Minh City. *Cai Luong* story lines tend to feature characters drawn from real life, setting it apart from the Chinese dramas upon which it is based, which portray the trials of gods and heroes. Developed in South Vietnam around 1920, *Cai Luong* is dismissed as highly sentimental by many Vietnamese, though it still draws large crowds in the countryside. *Photo by Catherine Karnow, USA*

FERMENTED RICE-MASH, DILUTED WITH water and drunk through bamboo straws, accompanies traditional dancing among the Black Thai minority of the central highlands. The liquor, which tastes like burnt grain, requires four or five days to reach full strength. It is customary to suck the fluid to the mouth of the tube and then, with the thumb held over the end, present it to a guest, who takes a short suck and hands it back.

Photo by Pham Tien Dung, Vietnam

FRIENDS SHARE A TOAST AND AN EVENING hot pot at an open-air café in the city of Lang Son, Lang Son Province. This soldier is one of the many military personnel in the area, which forms part of the border with China.

Photo by David Hume Kennerly, USA

HOPING TO WIN A TENT-BUILDING COMPE-
tition in Nghe An, Ho Chi Minh's native
province, a team of boys and girls prominently
display his portrait. The contest teaches
cleanliness, unity, and survival skills.
Photo by Tara Sosrowardoyo, Indonesia

MOVIE PRODUCERS AND THEIR ENTOURAGES
view daily rushes at the Hanoi Film Studios.
Not surprisingly, war and its aftermath are the
common themes in this growing industry.
Although some films are still weighed down by
propaganda, an increasing number challenge the
traditional boundaries governing free expression, artistic license, and political censorship.
Photo by Robin Moyer, USA

FRENCH TOURISTS RELIVE VIETNAM'S PAST
at a so-called "Royal Banquet" in Hue's Century
Hotel. The hotel is owned and managed by
Nguyen Phuoc Bao Hien, the grandson of
Emperor Thanh Thai, who sat on the throne
from 1889 until 1907. These guests have paid
to attend a special banquet at which they
get to put on royal robes and act out the roles
of Vietnamese nobility.
Photo by Monica Almeida, USA

THE FLOOR SHOW GETS UNDERWAY AT A
nightclub in Ho Chi Minh City. After a fast,
furious demonstration of disco dancing, these
two will do a little tumbling, and, for good
measure, a brief contortion act. Then they'll
yield the floor to the paying customers,
pack their bags, and head off to another club,
where they will repeat their routine.
Photo by Paul Chesley, USA

AT A NIGHT MARKET IN HAIPHONG,
bare bulbs light up the produce. As the
economy opens up, Vietnamese everywhere
are hustling to take advantage of the
potential for prosperity. Shopkeepers will
stay open all night if they think it might
bring in a little extra money.
Photo by P.F. Bentley, USA

CHANGING OF THE GUARD AT HO CHI MINH'S
Mausoleum in Hanoi. Ho's body lies in a glass
sarcophagus deep within this building, where an
elite military regiment stands guard as visitors
file past his body. In his will, Ho asked to be
cremated and that his ashes be buried in north,
south, and central Vietnam. Some Hanoians say
that someday that may happen, but in the
meantime, Ho's resting place doubles as a shrine
for the people and a symbol of authority for
those who rule. The former remember Ho as
Bac, or "Uncle," a man who loved children and
led his nation to freedom, while the latter rely on
his memory to help them hold on to power. Few
shifts in policy come without some suggestion
that Ho would have approved.
Photo by Robin Moyer, USA

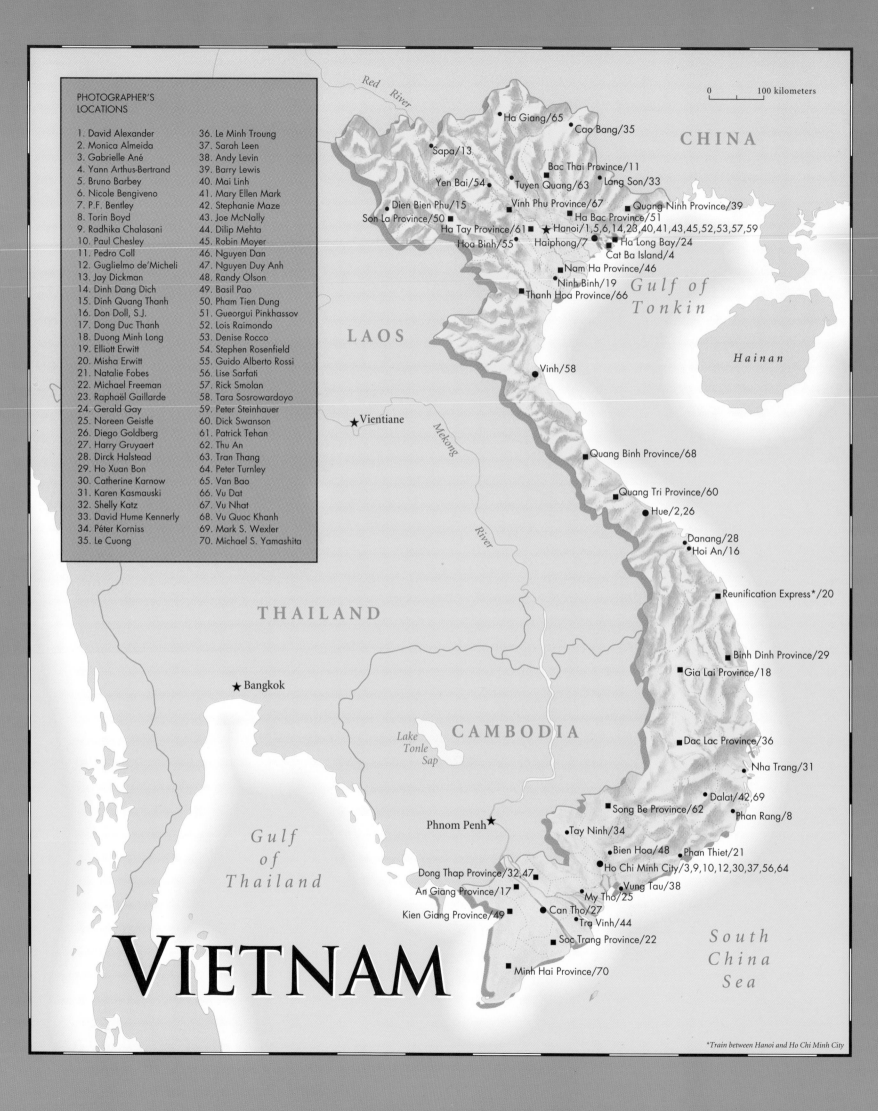

PHOTOGRAPHER'S LOCATIONS

1. David Alexander
2. Monica Almeida
3. Gabrielle Ané
4. Yann Arthus-Bertrand
5. Bruno Barbey
6. Nicole Bengiveno
7. P.F. Bentley
8. Torin Boyd
9. Radhika Chalasani
10. Paul Chesley
11. Pedro Coll
12. Guglielmo de'Micheli
13. Jay Dickman
14. Dinh Dang Dich
15. Dinh Quang Thanh
16. Don Doll, S.J.
17. Dong Duc Thanh
18. Duong Minh Long
19. Elliott Erwitt
20. Misha Erwitt
21. Natalie Fobes
22. Michael Freeman
23. Raphaël Gaillarde
24. Gerald Gay
25. Noreen Geistle
26. Diego Goldberg
27. Harry Gruyaert
28. Dirck Halstead
29. Ho Xuan Bon
30. Catherine Karnow
31. Karen Kasmauski
32. Shelly Katz
33. David Hume Kennerly
34. Péter Korniss
35. Le Cuong

36. Le Minh Troung
37. Sarah Leen
38. Andy Levin
39. Barry Lewis
40. Mai Linh
41. Mary Ellen Mark
42. Stephanie Maze
43. Joe McNally
44. Dilip Mehta
45. Robin Moyer
46. Nguyen Dan
47. Nguyen Duy Anh
48. Randy Olson
49. Basil Pao
50. Pham Tien Dung
51. Gueorgui Pinkhassov
52. Lois Raimondo
53. Denise Rocco
54. Stephen Rosenfield
55. Guido Alberto Rossi
56. Lise Sarfati
57. Rick Smolan
58. Tara Sosrowardoyo
59. Peter Steinhauer
60. Dick Swanson
61. Patrick Tehan
62. Thu An
63. Tran Thang
64. Peter Turnley
65. Van Bao
66. Vu Dat
67. Vu Nhat
68. Vu Quoc Khanh
69. Mark S. Wexler
70. Michael S. Yamashita

CHINA

Ha Giang/65
Cao Bang/35
Sapa/13
Bac Thai Province/11
Lang Son/33
Yen Bai/54
Tuyen Quang/63
Vinh Phu Province/67
Quang Ninh Province/39
Dien Bien Phu/15
Ha Bac Province/51
Son La Province/50
Ha Tay Province/61
Hanoi/1,5,6,14,23,40,41,43,45,52,53,57,59
Hoa Binh/55
Haiphong/7
Ha Long Bay/24
Cat Ba Island/4
Nam Ha Province/46
Ninh Binh/19
Gulf of Tonkin
Thanh Hoa Province/66

LAOS

★ Vientiane

Mekong

Vinh/58

Hainan

River

Quang Binh Province/68

Quang Tri Province/60
Hue/2,26

Danang/28
Hoi An/16

Reunification Express*/20

THAILAND

★ Bangkok

Binh Dinh Province/29

Gia Lai Province/18

CAMBODIA

Lake Tonle Sap

Dac Lac Province/36

Nha Trang/31

Dalat/42,69

Song Be Province/62

Phan Rang/8

Phnom Penh ★

Tay Ninh/34

Phan Thiet/21

Bien Hoa/48

Ho Chi Minh City/3,9,10,12,30,37,56,64

Gulf of Thailand

Dong Thap Province/32,47

Vung Tau/38

An Giang Province/17

My Tho/25

Kien Giang Province/49

Can Tho/27

Tra Vinh/44

Soc Trang Province/22

South China Sea

Minh Hai Province/70

VIETNAM

*Train between Hanoi and Ho Chi Minh City

0   100 kilometers

Photographer's Biographies

David Alexander, American
After devoting twenty years to photography for the recording and film industries, Alexander shifted directions and began creating montages constructed from black-and-white street photography. He is an owner of A&I Color Labs in Los Angeles.

Monica Almeida, American
Almeida began her career at the *Los Angeles Times* as part of the team of journalists awarded the 1984 Pulitzer Prize for coverage of California's Hispanic community. In 1986, she joined the staff of the *New York Daily News*, where she remained until 1991. She presently shoots for the *New York Times*.

Yann Arthus-Bertrand, French
One of the world's pre-eminent aerial photographers, Paris-based Arthus-Bertrand has published more than 40 titles, including aerial studies of Venice, Kenya, Egypt, Morocco, Paris, and numerous other regions of France. His work has appeared in *Life*, *National Geographic*, *GEO*, *Paris-Match*, *Figaro*, and many other European and American publications.

Bruno Barbey, French
Born in Morocco, Paris-based Barbey is a member of the Magnum photo agency. Since the early 1960s, he has worked on assignments throughout the world, producing stories in Biafra, Vietnam, Chile, and Kuwait. He has published seven books of his own work. His work has been exhibited in Paris, London, Rome, and Zurich.

Nicole Bengiveno, American
A staff member of the *New York Daily News* for eight years, Bengiveno received first-place awards in 1987 and 1989 from the New York Associated Press for her feature photography from the Soviet Union. Before moving to New York, she shot for the *San Francisco Examiner* for eight years, during which time she was named Bay Area Press Photographer of the Year, in 1979. Based in New York City, she is affiliated with the Matrix photo agency.

P.F. Bentley, American
P.F. Bentley has been a photographer for *Time* magazine for the past fifteen years. In 1984, 1988, and 1992, he received first-place awards in the National Press Photographers Pictures of the Year competition for his campaign coverage. He spent 1992 on the campaign trail with presidential candidate Bill Clinton, producing *Portrait of Victory*, a best-selling book and CD-ROM published by Warner Books.

Torin Boyd, American
Now based in Tokyo, Boyd began his career as a surfing photographer in Cocoa Beach, Florida. He has contributed to *Fortune*, *Newsweek*, *Time*, and *U.S. News & World Report*, where he is a staff photographer.

Radhika Chalasani, American
A native New Yorker, Chalasani has lived in Ho Chi Minh City since 1993. Before that, she was based in Hong Kong, where she shot for the Agence France-Press. Affiliated with the Gamma-Liaison photo agency, her work has appeared in *Time*, *Newsweek*, and *U.S. News & World Report*.

Paul Chesley, American
As a freelancer for *National Geographic* magazine, Chesley has completed 35 projects worldwide. Solo exhibitions of his work have appeared in museums in London, Tokyo, New York, and Honolulu. His work has appeared in *Life*, *Fortune*, *GEO*, *Newsweek*, and *Time*. He presently lives in Aspen, Colorado.

Pedro Coll, Spanish
Coll abandoned a career as a lawyer at the age of 28 to pursue photography, and has since traveled on assignment to five continents. He specializes in travel and editorial work. Based in Palma de Mallorca, Spain, he is represented by agencies in Barcelona, London, Frankfurt, New York, Milan, Paris, Tokyo, and Melbourne.

Guglielmo de' Micheli, Italian
Based in Florence, de' Micheli is a regular contributor to the Italian magazines *Capital* and *7 Sette*, as well as the American publications *Sports Illustrated* and *Forbes*. He has also contributed to *Life* and *Time* and has participated in numerous *Day in the Life* projects.

Jay Dickman, American
Winner of the 1983 Pulitzer Prize and a gold medalist in the World Press Photo Foundation competition, Dickman is a freelancer based in Denver. His work appears in *Time*, *Life*, *GEO*, *National Geographic*, and *Stern*.

Dinh Quang Thanh, Vietnamese
Dinh Quang Thanh has received twenty prizes for art and journalism, including one international Silver Prize and two Copper Prizes. A member of the Vietnamese Photographers Association, he has participated in numerous exhibitions, including one of his personal work, which appeared at the Vietnam News Agency. He presently lives in Hanoi.

Don Doll, S.J., American
From his base at Creighton University in Omaha, Nebraska, Doll has produced numerous stories about Native American life. Two stories about Eskimos have been published by *National Geographic*. Crown Publishers recently released his book, *Vision Quest: Men, Women, and Sacred Sites of the Sioux Nation*.

Dong Duc Thanh, Vietnamese
A photographer for the *Youth Newspaper*, Dong Duc Thanh has earned numerous medals both in his native country and abroad, including a Bronze Medal at an international exhibition sponsored in Italy by the International Federation of Photographic Art. He is a resident of Ho Chi Minh City and a member of the Vietnamese Photographers Association.

Duong Minh Long, Vietnamese
Born in 1962, Duong Minh Long has had personal exhibitions in Warsaw, Moscow, Hanoi, and Ho Chi Minh City. He presently shoots for *Labor Newspaper* in Ho Chi Minh City. In 1991, he published a collection of 30 of his own black-and-white photographs.

Elliott Erwitt, American
Born in Paris, raised in Milan, Erwitt moved to New York in 1948. There he met Robert Capa, who invited him to join the newly formed Magnum photo agency in 1953. He has published numerous books since then, including *Son of Bitch* and *Elliott Erwitt: Personal Exposures*. Exhibitions of his work have appeared at New York's Museum of Modern Art, the Smithsonian Institution, and the Museum of Modern Art in Paris.

Misha Erwitt, American
A native New Yorker, Erwitt began taking pictures ate age 11. His work has been published in *Time*, *Newsweek*, *Esquire*, the *New York Times Magazine*, and has participated in eight *Day in the Life* projects. He is presently on the staff of the *New York Daily News*.

Natalie Fobes, American
A freelancer based in Seattle, Fobes has built a specialty around photography of the ocean and its inhabitants. In 1988, she was awarded a Scripps-Howard Meeman award for a study she wrote and photographed about Pacific salmon. The book of that project, ten years in the making, was published in the fall of 1994 by Alaska Northwest. She has also received the prestigious Alicia Patterson Fellowship.

Michael Freeman, British
Freeman took an M.A. at Oxford and devoted six years to advertising before beginning a career as an editorial photographer. At first a contract photographer for Time-Life, he soon became *Smithsonian*'s principal contributor. The author of 24 books about photography, he re-

cently published two books of his own work, *Palaces of the Gods* and *Angkor: The Hidden Glories*. He is presently based in London.

Raphaël Gaillarde, French
A leading photographer with the Gamma Presse Images photo agency, Gaillarde's coverage of world events has appeared in magazines all over Europe, including *Paris-Match* and *GEO*. In 1990, he received World Press Photo's prestigious Oskar Barnack Award.

Gerald Gay, Australian
A native of Singapore, Gay specializes in fashion, food, interiors, and architecture. His photos have appeared in *Signature* and *Interior Digest*. He is a partner in Developing Agents Photography, an agency in Singapore.

Diego Goldberg, Argentine
Goldberg began his photographic career as a Latin American correspondent for Camera Press. In 1977, he moved to Paris and joined the Sygma photo agency. Now based in Buenos Aires, he received a World Press Photo Foundation award in 1984. In the past two years, he has acted as a judge for World Press Photo and the W. Eugene Smith Grant Foundation.

Harry Gruyaert, Belgian
A recipient of the 1976 Kodak Prize for color photography, Gruyaert has been a member of the Magnum photo agency since 1981. Based in Paris, he has published several books, including *Lumières Blanches* and *Morocco*. He has exhibited all over Europe and the U.S.

Dirck Halstead, American
Through six administrations, Halstead has covered the White House for *Time* magazine. He has photographed a record 47 covers for *Time* since 1972. Before then, he worked for UPI in Saigon, where he opened its Vietnamese bureau. In 1975, he won the Overseas Press Club's Robert Capa Gold Medal for his coverage of the collapse of South Vietnam. He is based in Washington, D.C.

Prime Minister Vo Van Kiet and Passage to Vietnam *Director Rick Smolan. Photo by P.F. Bentley*

Italian photographer Guglielmo de' Micheli hits the streets in Ho Chi Minh City. Photo by Catherine Karnow

Ho Xuan Bon, Vietnamese
A resident of Danang, Ho Xuan Bon has received many awards for his work, including one from the Asian Cultural Center of UNESCO. He is a member of the Vietnamese Photographers Association.

Catherine Karnow, American
Born in Hong Kong, Karnow has photographed extensively in Vietnam, France, Scotland, and the Caribbean. Her work appears regularly in *Smithsonian*, *GEO*, *Islands*, as well as numerous other magazines and books. Affiliated with the Woodfin Camp photo agency, she presently lives in San Francisco.

Karen Kasmauski, American
Before joining *National Geographic* in 1984, Kasmauski was a member of the staff of the *Virginian-Pilot/Ledger Star* in Norfolk, Virginia. At the *Geographic*, she has produced stories about radiation, Japanese women, viruses, and Japan's economic role in Asia. She has won two awards at the Pictures of the Year competition, one for her coverage of radiation, the other for a story on Down's syndrome.

Shelly Katz, American
Born and raised in New York City, Shelly Katz sold his first pictures to the *New York Daily News* at the age of 12. In 1961, he joined the U.S. Air Force and spent four years photographing for the military, fulfilling several tours of duty in Vietnam. He is presently based in Dallas, Texas, where he works as a contributing photographer for *Time*.

David Hume Kennerly, American
Awarded the Pulitzer Prize for his work in Vietnam, David Hume Kennerly has covered stories in 130 countries for UPI, *Life* and *Time* magazines. He was the personal photographer to President Gerald R. Ford from 1974 to 1977 and has produced several feature-length films about his experiences as a photojournalist. He has been awarded many of photography's most prestigious honors, including two World Press Photo Foundation first place awards and the Overseas Press Club's Olivier Rebbot Award for best reporting from abroad.

Péter Korniss, Hungarian
A freelancer based in Budapest, Korniss began his career as a dance photographer. He subsequently devoted 15 years to documenting the vanishing traditions of Eastern Europe's peasantry and ten years to photographing the lifestyles of migrant workers in Hungary, for which he won a World Press Photo award.

Le Cuong, Vietnamese
Based in Hanoi, Le Cuong has participated in exhibitions in Germany, France, Japan, Russia, Romania, and Iraq. He has collaborated in several books on Vietnamese culture and has received awards both at home and abroad for his work. He is a member of the Vietnamese Photographers Association.

Le Minh Truong, Vietnamese
Le Minh Truong has had four personal exhibitions in Hanoi, Ho Chi Minh City and other locales. In 1969 and 1971, he won first prize in the National Photography Exhibition for stories about cement and Vietnam's Long Range Mountains. He is a member of the Vietnamese Photographers Association.

Sarah Leen, American
Born in Wisconsin, raised as an Army brat in Canada, Europe, and the U.S., Leen began her career at the *Arizona Daily Star*, in Tuscon, Arizona. After five years at the *Philadelphia Inquirer*, she joined Matrix, a photo agency in New York. She has produced stories for the *National Geographic* about Alaska, California, Canada, and Siberia. Her work has also appeared in *Time*, *GEO*, *Audubon*, and the *London Daily Telegraph Sunday Magazine*. She presently lives in Arlington, Virginia.

Andy Levin, American
A contributing photographer to *Life* magazine, Levin is a freelancer based in New York City, where he is currently at work on a long-term project about Coney Island. In 1985, he received first prize in the National Press Photographers Association Pictures of the Year competition for an essay on a Nebraska farm family. A 1986 story on the Statue of Liberty earned the same prize.

Barry Lewis, British
A founder of the Network Photo Agency in London, Lewis's work has been published and exhibited widely in his native England. In 1991, he won World Press Photo's Oskar Barnack Award for his work in Romania. His work regularly appears in the *London Sunday Times Magazine*, *Life*, *GEO*, *Fortune*, and *Newsweek*.

Mary Ellen Mark, American
One of the most celebrated photographers of our time, Mark has been awarded three fellowships from the National Endowment for the Arts, two Robert F. Kennedy Awards and, most recently, a Guggenheim Fellowship. A retrospective of her work, entitled *Mary Ellen Mark: Twenty Five Years*, was published in 1991 by the New York Graphic Society. An exhibit of photographs from the same collection is in the midst of an international tour.

Stephanie Maze, American
A winner of a first-place award from the White House Press Photographers Association in 1985, Maze freelances as both a photographer and picture editor out of her home in Washington, D.C. She is the founder of Maze Productions, which specializes in photographic projects for children. She has produced numerous stories for *National Geographic* and many other publications in Europe and America.

Joe McNally, American
After starting out at the *New York Daily News*, McNally spent two years as a still photographer for ABC-TV. He has freelanced for magazines since 1981, publishing primarily for *Life*, *National Geographic*, and *Sports Illustrated*. He is affiliated with Sygma and works out of his home in Hastings, New York.

Dilip Mehta, Canadian
An original member of Contact Press Images, Mehta has worked extensively in his native India, covering the aftermath of Indira Gandhi's assassination and the Bhopal chemical spill—work for which he was awarded World Press Photo Foundation Awards in 1985. His photos have appeared in the *New York Times Magazine*, *Paris-Match*, the *London Sunday Times Magazine*, and *National Geographic*. He lives with his wife and son in New Delhi, India.

Robin Moyer, American
A contract photographer for *Time* based in Hong Kong, Moyer has won many of photography's most prestigious awards, including the World Press Photo Foundation's Press Photo of the Year and the Overseas Press Club's Robert Capa Gold Medal for his coverage of the 1983 conflict in Lebanon.

Nguyen Dan, Vietnamese
A graduate of the University of Commerce, Nguyen Dan is a former correspondent of the newspaper *Trade*. His work has been widely exhibited and has earned prizes both at home and abroad. He is a member of the Vietnamese Photographers Association.

Nguyen Duy Anh, Vietnamese
A two-time winner of prizes from the Asian Cultural Center of UNESCO, Nguyen Duy Anh has been honored for both his artistic and journalistic work. In 1991, he received a National Press Prize as well as two Golden Medals for Artistic Photography. He is a member of the Vietnamese Photographers Association.

Randy Olson, American
A freelancer based near Pittsburgh, Pennsylvania, Olson received the Newspaper Photographer of the Year award in 1992. In the preceding year, he was honored with the Robert F. Kennedy Award for photojournalism. His work has appeared in *National Geographic*, *Fortune*, *Life*, and *U.S. News & World Report*.

Basil Pao, Hong Kong
Pao began his extensive career in New York in 1973, working in Hong Kong, Los Angeles, and New York as a designer, art director, writer, and producer before deciding to concentrate on photography in 1986. His photographs of Bertolucci's *The Last Emperor*—a film on which he served as assistant director—have been published in U.S. and Asian magazines.

Pham Tien Dung, Vietnamese
A graduate of the Journalism Faculty of the former USSR, Pham Tien Dung presently shoots for *Vietnam Pictorial*. He is a resident of Hanoi and a member of the Vietnamese Photographers Association.

Hungarian photographer Péter Korniss was assigned to photograph the Holy See of the Cao Dai faith in Long Thanh, Tay Ninh Province. Photo by Péter Korniss

Gueorgui Pinkhassov, French
Born and raised in the former USSR, Pinkhassov served as an assistant in Moscow's Mosfilm studios until 1985, when he became an independent photojournalist. He emigrated to Paris in 1985, where he joined the Magnum photo agency in 1988.

Lois Raimondo, American
A resident of Hanoi, Raimondo has been working in Asia for more than six years. She has published one book, *The Little Lama of Tibet*, and her work has appeared in *Life*, the *New York Times*, *Der Spiegel*, and *Paris-Match*. In 1988, she was a finalist in voting for the Pulitzer Prize for her investigative reporting.

Denise Rocco, American
A documentary photographer, Rocco received a grant from the Polaroid Corporation to photograph in the public housing developments of Boston. Her work has appeared in *American Photo Magazine* and exhibited at New York's Lumina Art Gallery. She presently lives in Sausalito, California.

Guido Alberto Rossi, Italian
Born in Milan in 1949, Rossi is the owner of Image Bank Italy. For many years, he covered the Middle East and Indochina. A certified pilot, he specializes in aerial photography, as well as sports and travel. He is based in Milan.

Lise Sarfati, French
Based in Moscow, Sarfati has spent the last few years traveling throughout the former Soviet Union, documenting the societal shifts occasioned by the fall of communism. She has produced stories on runaway children, transsexuals and the Don Cossacks. She is affiliated with the photo agency Contact Press Images.

Rick Smolan, American
The creator of the *Day in the Life* series, Smolan is the co-director, along with his wife Jennifer Erwitt, of *Passage to Vietnam*. He was a founding member of the photo agency Contact Press Images and one of *Time* magazine's chief photographers in Asia and Australia. He presently lives in Northern California.

Tara Sosrowardoyo, Indonesian
Born in New York, Sosrowardoyo began his career as a still photographer for feature films. Now a freelancer based in Jakarta, he produces everything from album covers to editorial and advertising work. His photos have appeared in the *New York Times*, *Time*, and *Vogue Paris*.

Peter Steinhauer, American
A resident of Hanoi since December, 1993, Steinhauer is the son of a naval surgeon who served in the 3rd Marine Division in Danang from 1966 to 1967. A recent graduate of the Colorado Institute of Art, he is presently at work on a black-and-white study of the faces and landscapes of Vietnam.

Dick Swanson, American
In 1966, Swanson went to Vietnam to cover the war for *Life*. In 1971, he became the magazine's White House photographer and continues to work out of Washington, producing stories for *Time*, *National Geographic*, *Newsweek*, and the *Washington Post*. His work is included in

At the end of the Passage to Vietnam *shoot week, American photographer David Hume Kennerly married Rebecca Soladay in a ceremony inside the Hanoi Opera House. Photo by Shelly Katz*

MoMa's permanent collection and he has received awards from the World Press Photo Foundation, the National Press Photographers Association, and the White House Press Photographers Association.

Patrick Tehan, American
Formerly with the *Orange County Register* and the *Pittsburgh Press*, Tehan was runner-up in the 1992 Newspaper Photographer of the Year award. He is currently the director of photography at the *Sun*, in Bremerton, Washington.

Thu An, Vietnamese
Born in Nhatrang in 1944, Thu An has received awards from all around the world, including ones from Poland, Russia, and Japan. In 1989, the Asian Cultural Center of UNESCO awarded him its Grand Prize. He is a member of the Vietnamese Photographers Association.

Tran Thang, Vietnamese
Educated at the University of Journalism, Tran Thang has won Vietnam's National Prize as well as Mongolia's Prize for photography. A member of the Vietnamese Photographers Association, his work has been exhibited twice, in 1990 and 1991. He is a resident of Ho Chi Minh City.

Peter Turnley, American
A contract photographer for *Newsweek*, Turnley's work is distributed by the Black Star photo agency. For the past ten years, he has covered the world's news events. He has won numerous international awards, including the Overseas Press Club Award for the best photoreporting from abroad. He is based in Paris.

Van Bao, Vietnamese
One of the most highly respected photographers in Vietnam, Van Bao is Deputy Secretary General of the Vietnamese Photographers Association. He received an international Gold Medal in 1989, in conjunction with the 150th anniversary of photography.

Vu Dat, Vietnamese
A lieutenant colonel in the Vietnamese Army, Vu Dat received a first prize from the Ministry of National Defense in 1992 for his work. A resident of Hanoi, he is a member of the Vietnamese Photographers Association.

Vu Nhat, Vietnamese
A member of the Vietnamese Photographers Association, Vu Nhat has won two first prizes and two second prizes in Hanoi's Artistic Photo Contest. He has also received the Ho Guom Prize for the body of work he produced during the years 1987 to 1992.

Vu Quoc Khanh, Vietnamese
A graduate of the Photographic University in the former German Democratic Republic, Vu Quoc Khanh won a special prize for a work entitled, "Mother's Sun." Based in Hanoi, he recently took part in an exhibition, "Vietnamese Children and Our Concern." He is a member of the Vietnamese Photographers Association.

Mark S. Wexler, American
Wexler has covered such diverse topics as the American South for *National Geographic* and Japanese youth for *Smithsonian*. He won three World Press Awards for his work on a *Day in the Life of Japan*. His book, *Los Angeles*, was published in the summer of 1994. He recently moved to Chicago.

Michael S. Yamashita, American
Yamashita spends six months of the year on the road, shooting for a variety of clients. He has been a regular contributor to *National Geographic* since 1979. For his most recent story on the Mekong River, he visited China, Myanmar, Laos, Thailand, Cambodia, and Vietnam. Affiliated with the Woodfin Camp photo agency, he lives in New Jersey.

Writers' Biographies

Pico Iyer
A long-time essayist for *Time*, Pico Iyer is the author of *Video Night in Kathmandu*, *The Lady and the Monk*, and *Falling off the Map*. He has just completed a novel set in Cuba.

Stanley Karnow
Stanley Karnow, author of *Vietnam: A History*, earned six Emmys as chief correspondent of the PBS Series, *Vietnam: A Television History*. In 1990, his book *In Our Image: America's Empire in the Philippines* earned him the Pulitzer Prize in history.

Colin Leinster
A member of the Board of Editors at *Fortune*, Colin Leinster has a 27-year relationship with Vietnam. He ran the *Life* bureau in Saigon from 1967 to 1969 and returned to the country in 1988, shortly after economic liberalization. He is the author of *The Outsider*, a novel which Paramount produced as a movie. Married with one child, he is based in New York City.

Peter Saidel
Peter Saidel is an editor at the *Vietnam Investment Review* in Hanoi. He has lived in Hanoi and Ho Chi Minh City for the past three years.

GOLD SPONSORS

Apple Computer, Inc. headquartered in Cupertino, California, develops, manufactures and markets personal computer, server, and personal interactive electronic systems and services for use in a wide range of markets. A recognized pioneer and innovator in high-technology products, Apple does business in more than 120 countries. It seeks, through technology, to provide people with easy and affordable access to information and computing power.

Eastman Kodak Company, the world leader in photography, produces films, papers and chemicals for professional and amateur use; electronic imaging products; motion picture films; copier-duplicators; and hundreds of other products for business and industry, health care and the home. The company employs more than 110,000 people worldwide, 57,000 of them in the U.S. In 1993, Kodak revenues totaled more than 16.4 billion dollars, with nearly half coming from sales outside the U.S.

Thai Airways International, the national carrier of the Kingdom of Thailand, is one of the most successful airlines in the world today.

Established in 1960, Thai presently operates a fleet of over 65 ultra-modern, wide-bodied jets to more than 70 world-wide destinations across 35 countries.

The company employs 20,000 people. It has posted profits in each of the last 29 years, making it virtually unique within the airline industry.

Thai Farmers Bank is the second largest bank in Thailand in terms of total assets. As of December 31, 1993, its total assets were US$17.3 billion and its net profit was US$312 million, up by 52.4% from the previous year versus the 40.7% rate of growth of the entire banking system. At present, the bank has 436 domestic branches and nine overseas branches. In November, 1993, Thai Farmers Bank became the first private establishment in Thailand to be given an "AAA" rating by the Thai Rating and Information Service Co., Ltd (TRIS).

The Regent, Bangkok is famed for its accessible location on Rajadamri Road. The exquisite lobby, with its ceiling of hand-painted silk is the perfect place to conduct business or relax. The 400 luxurious guestrooms include 32 suites and 7 private cabanas. All have a spacious bathroom, amenities and separate dressing area. Exotic greenery decorates the courtyards and gardens. The Business Centre, ballroom and eight function rooms meet every business need. A pool, squash courts and health centre offer relaxing diversions.

Nestlé Thailand Ltd.—In 1867, Henri Nestlé created the first infant formula in Switzerland. While the original business was based on milk and dietetic foods, numerous other products have been added to the line over the years: chocolate, culinary, ice cream, mineral water and pet foods.

From 15 factories in 1900 to 489 today, Nestlé has long been known worldwide, and certain flagship products, like Nescafé, are sold in more than 100 countries.

Federal Express is delighted and proud to be the official air express service of *Passage to Vietnam*. Employing more than 100,000 people worldwide, Federal Express is the world's largest air express transportation company, providing fast and reliable services for important documents, packages and freight.

Currently, Federal Express ships to over 185 countries and delivers more than 2 million items every day. We are proud of this achievement and will continue our commitment to serve our customers with excellence.

A photograph is no longer a two dimensional object. Today it can be stored forever on disc, transmitted electronically anywhere in the world, and seamlessly altered or combined. It can be simultaneously analyzed, edited and manipulated in different parts of the country, and reproduced in an almost infinite variety of ways. In other words, photography has changed forever. At A&I Color and ZZYZX Visual Systems, we are part of that change. Using traditional chemical processing, A&I gives professional photographers the advantage of starting with the highest quality film or print image. Then through the digital imaging services of ZZYZX, we are able to store, transmit, enhance and reproduce whatever is desired. A&I and ZZYZX are dedicated to providing the most useful and advanced services to photographers and their clients.

Motorola is one of the world's leading providers of wireless communications, semiconductors and advanced electronic systems and services. Major equipment businesses include cellular telephone, two-way radio, paging and data communications, personal communications, automotive, defense and space electronics and computers. Communication devices, computers and millions of consumer products are powered by Motorola semiconductors. The company maintains sales, service and manufacturing facilities throughout the world, conducts business on six continents and employs approximately 120,000 people worldwide.

Founded in 1992 by Paul Allen and David E. Liddle, Interval Research Corporation performs research and advanced development in areas of information systems, communications and computer science. The company emphasizes work in a number of pre-competitive technologies requiring more research to determine commercial potential; and collaborates with other research groups and university laboratories.

Interval believes that the emergence of high-capacity, low-cost ubiquitous communications during the coming decade will profoundly change the opportunities for creative use of information and stimulate new approaches to organizing knowledge and human interactions with information-rich products and services.

SILVER SPONSORS

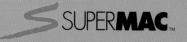

SuperMac Technology is a leading supplier of high-performance peripherals and subsystems for the desktop color-publishing, digital photography, and digital-video markets. Our products are designed to provide Macintosh, Power Macintosh, and Windows users with the industry's best graphics performance, highest-quality color, and most complete feature offerings. For professionals who communicate through print or video, Supermac's graphics and digital-video cards, large-screen displays, and printers deliver professional-quality results.

A specialized manufacturer of optics for various applications for over 45 years, Tamron Industries, Inc. is a major supplier of exotic lenses and ground-breaking technologies designed to bring high quality lenses to all photo enthusiasts. With the introduction of its Fotovix line in 1986, Tamron entered the digital revolution by bridging traditional silver-halide photography to electronics. The company also makes a wide array of lenses for CCTV applications.

XEROX

Xerox Corporation is a global enterprise serving the worldwide document processing market. The company offers a full range of Xerox copiers, duplicators, digital production publishers, electronic printers, facsimiles, scanners, computer software, supplies and a growing array of color products to over 130 countries.

A worldwide network of research centers provides Xerox with technological excellence in supporting growing business opportunities.

Xerox, The Document Company, is dedicated to providing quality products and services that deliver the highest possible levels of customer satisfaction.

Major Contributors

ad·hoc INTERACTIVE
Adobe Systems
Aldus Corporation
Applied Graphics Technologies
Articulate Systems
Berkeley Systems
Books that Work
Broderbund Software
CE Software Inc.
CKS Partners
Claris Corporation
Common Knowledge Inc.
Creative Multimedia
Cyan Inc.
DayStar Digital Inc.
FWB Incorporated
Global Village Communications
Hewlett Packard
HFC Software
Intermagic
Intuit
Iomega Corporation
Living Books
NewGen Systems Corporation
Now Software Inc.
Pallas Photo
Photo Impact
Photonics Corporation
Pinnacle Effects
Publishers Group West
Radius, Inc.
Rémy Martin Cognac
Sahaviriya Systems
San Francisco Production Group
Shiva Corporation
Symantec Corporation
Technöggin
Virtus Corporation
Xerox Corporation
Zzyzx Visual Systems

Black Star Publishing
Blockbuster Video
Body Shop International
Buzz Magazine
Canon USA Inc.
Carbone Smolan Associates
Cathay Pacific Airways Ltd.
Cheskin + Masten
Chronicle Books
Clement Mok Designs
Communication Arts Magazine
Cone Communications
Contact Press Images
Creative Artists Agency
Criswell Communications
Crystal Dynamics
Cunningham Communications
Dae Advertising
Daedalus Books
Eden Interactive
Elephant Productions
Excella Travel Ltd.
Farallon Computing, Inc.
Fortune Magazine
FPG International
Friday Holdings
Gamma Liaison
General Magic
Germaine's Restaurant
Graphics Resource
Hotel Sofitel Metropole
ICM
Imagine Films
Institute for the Future
Institutional Incorporated Partners
International Center of Photography
Interval Research
Iuppa McCartan Inc.
Just Film
Life Magazine
Light Source Computer Images Inc.
MacConnection
Macromedia
Macweek
Macworld
Magnus, Nankervis, Curl & Howard
Marin Litho
McClean Public Relations
Micro Publishing News
Microsoft Corporation
Midem Organization
Nash Editions
National Geographic Society
The New Lab
New Media Magazine
The New York Times
News Photographer Magazine
Newsweek Magazine
Nikon Inc.
Olympus Camera
Opera News
Parke-Davis
People Magazine
Photo District News
Photo Perspectives

PhotoSource International
Pop Rocket
Portfolio Systems
Provider Company
PSF Transcription
Putnam New Media
Quark Inc.
Redgate Communications
Reportáge
Rosewood Stone Group
San Francisco Focus
Santa Fe Photographic Workshops
Schering Plough Pharmaceutical
Seybold Publications
Sheil Land Associates
Sheila Donnelly & Associates
Social Venture Network
Sony Corporation of America
Stanford Alumni Association
Sushi Ran
Sygma Photo
Tiburon Lodge
Time Magazine
Timestream Inc.
TONBO Designs
Tower Books
Transpac
Tut Systems
United Airlines
United Digital Artists
Universal Press Syndicate
USA Today
Userland Software
Utne Reader
Videomation
Vietnam Airlines
Vietnam Investment Review
Vietnam Today
Vietnamese Association of
    Photographic Artists
Virgin Airlines
Vivid Publishing Inc.
The Wall Street Journal
The Washington Post
Waterside Productions
Weldon Owen Publishing
Whole Earth Review
Wildfire Communications
Wired Magazine
Woodrum Marine
Xunhasaba Guesthouse

Contributors

Adam Software
Alex Brown & Sons
Ambrosia Software
America Online
American Express
American Photo Magazine
American Zoetrope
Animatrix
Antique Timepieces
ANZ Bank, Hanoi
Arnowitz Associates
Art Center College of Design
Arts & Communication Counselors
Asia, Inc.
Associated Press
Australian Mission to the U.N.
Baker & McKenzie, Hong Kong
Balestra Capital
Bank of America
Bill Communications

FRIENDS AND ADVISORS

Kanok Abhiradee
Dan Adler
Philippe Agret
Vin Alabiso
Mitch Albom
Rhoda & Ira Albom
Stewart Alsop
John & Rebecca Altberg
An Pham Xuan Hoang
Jane Anderson
Nathalie Ané
Burt Arnowitz
Lois Artz
Liz Arum
Rea Ashley
Bill Atkinson
Chris August
Susan Baden-Powell
John Baker
Sarah Bales
Fred Barber
Peter Baren
Andrew & Lissa Barnum
Ed & Rena Barnum
Lori Barra
Tom Barwick
Mary K. Bauman
Jane Bay
Rudy Becks
Martin Beeman
Jeff Berg
Gussie Bergerman
Richard Bernstein
Nicholas & James Berube
Bich Hanh
Michel Birnbaum
Lori Birtley
Bill Black
Susan Bloom
Ina Blumberg
Mike Boettcher
David Bohrman
Bob Bombino
Amy Bonetti
James Botton
Phillipe Bouissou
Tony Bové
Kathy Bower
Emily Boxer
Jessica Brackman
Fred Brady
Paul Brainerd
Joe Brancatelli
Cappel Brand
Donald Brenner
Bridgit Brewer
Marshall & Nina Brickman
Batong Briones
David Brown
Margot Brown
Russell Brown
Jackson Browne
Clark Brownstein
Hal Buell
Emma Bufton
Jane Bunch
John Bundy
Al & Dawn Bunetta
David Bunnell
Phil Burfurd
Fred Burke
David & Iris Burnett

Arnold Burns
Diane Burns
Red Burns
Diana Butler
Richard Butler
Dave Butz
Liz & Gerry Byrne
Linda Caine
Sean Callahan
Nicholas & Yukine Callaway
Bill Campbell
Elise Cannon
Devora Canter
Marc Canter
Cornell & Edith Capa
Steve Capps
Ken & Janet Carbone
Chris Cardwell
David Carriere
Helen Carrigan
Clive Cartwright
Denise Caruso
Steve Case
Frank Catchpool
Barbara Cavalier
Jim Cavuto
Linda Celko
Mike & Gina Cerre
Sussy Chako
Stephen Chao
Ian & Marjorie Chapman
Tom Chapman
Howard & Jeanette Chapnick
Harriett Choice
Albert Chu
Laurence Chu
Chu Minh Duc
Jim & Mary Cimino
RoseAnn Cimino-Schott
Jess & Rhoda Claman
Rich Clarkson
Andree & Josephine Clift
Margaret Clift
Shane & Megan Clift
Chuck Clifton
Gail Cohen
Ed Collier
Budd Colligan
Jimmy Colton
Don Conklin
Meryl Cook
Rob & Mary Anne Cook
Scott Cook
Guy Cooper
Francis Ford & Eleanor Coppola
Jack & Helen Corn
Vien Cortes
Laura Cox
Bob Cramer
Kim Criswell
Andie Cunningham
Richard Curtis
Barbara Custer
Heidi Cuttler
Marie D'Amico
Surinder Dahiya
Basel Dalloul
Dang The Truyen
Robyn Davidson
Jan Davis
Anne Day
Jerry De Avila

Cliff Deeds
Chris DeMoulin
Ray & Barbara DeMoulin
Alan Deutschman
Wongvipa Devahastin
David & Ann Devoss
Dinh Dinh Dang
Dinh Huyen Tram
Dinh Thu Huong
Robynne Dinkelaker
Doan Tuyet
Walter Dods
Ann Doherty
Jim Domke
Claire Donahue
Sheila Donnelly
Arnold Drapkin
Fred Drasner
Tony Driskell
Dick Duncan
Francine Duncan
Ken & Pam Duncan
Beverly Dunn
John & Eileen Dunn
Duong Duc Hong
John Durniak
Anoa Dussol
Esther Dyson
Soren Dyssegaard
Oscar Dystell
Fred Ebrahimi
Steve Edelman
Dan Eilers
Sandra Eisert
Kathleen Egge
Rohn & Jeri Engh
John Englehart
Michela English
David, Sheri, Erik & C.J. Erwitt
Ellen Erwitt
Jeanette Erwitt
Sasha & Amy Erwitt
George Esper
Steve Ettlinger
Gordon Eubanks
John Evans
Daniel & Elinore Farber
Roland Fasel
Peter Faucetta
Patti Felker
Bran Ferren
Janine Firpo
Peggy Fledderjohn
Randy Fleming
Marty Fox
Malcolm & Tammie Fraser
David Friend
Tom Fristoe
Ken Fromm
Elizabeth Frost
Fred Fuchs
Stuart Gaines
Marvin & Leslie Gans
Laurine Garaude
Jenny Garber
Lori Garrabrant
Sharon Garrett
Jean Louis Gassee
Susan Gates
Pamela Geismar
Andre P. van Gelderein
Stefanos Georgantis

Edouard George
Bill Getz
Edna Ghertler
Miles Gilburn
Rudolf Gildemeister
Tom & Peg Gildersleeve
Bob Gilka
Brendan Gill
Shannon Gilligan
Bill Gladstone
Sandy Gleysteen
Ira Glick
Nat & Marilyn Goldhaber
Lisa Goldman
Bernice Goldmark
Bob Goldstein
Andrew Golub
Mark Gordon
Joel Gottler
Eric J. Gould
Arty & Flo Grace
John Grant
Brian Grazer
Nancye Green
Jake & Cynthia Greenberg
George Greenfield
DeLois Greenwood
Gilbert M. Grosvenor
Holly Halford
F.L. Hamb
Sheryl Hamptom
Michelle Han
Eric Hangen
Gary Hare
Acey Harper
Gareth Harris
Nick & Jane Harris
Patricia Hartigan
Buzz Hartshorn
Roy Harvey
Michelle Hasson
Bob Hawke
John Hays
David Hazlett
Francois Hebel
Kate Heery
Ginny Heinlein
Greg & Pru Heisler
Carolyn Herter
Andy Hertzfeld
Murray Hiebert
James Higa
Paul Hilts
Hoang Thi Phuong Thao
Hoang Thinh
David Hodnett
Hans Hoefer
Gary Hoenig
Sam Hoffman
Nigel & Erin Holmes
Christina Holovach
Pat Holt
Nancy Hooff
Stacey Hoover
Will Hopkins
Ron Howard
Kerry Hubert
Suphot Hudakorn
Drew Huffman
Gary Hughes
Jim & Evelyn Hughes
Bill Hurst

Lindsey & Paul Iacovino
Christopher Ireland
Chuck & Carol Isaacs
Eiko Ishioka
Vern & Pigeon Iuppa
Rita D. Jacobs
Tom Jacobson
Bill James
Juanita James
Amy Janello
Mort Janklow
Doug Jerum
James Joaquin
Steve Jobs
Judith & Richard Johnson-Marsano
Brennon Jones
Randy Jones
Kim & Kim Kapin
Gabriella Karsch
Lan Kauffman
Bill Kelly
Kathleen Kennedy
Peter Kennedy
Brad Kibbel
George Kimble
Harry Kirchner
Michael & Veronica Kleeman
Kai Kraus
Michelle Kraus
J.P. & Eliane Laffont
Andrew Lam
Tony Lam
Linda Lamb
Banthoon Lamsam
Jim Lawton
Le Lan
Le Phuc
Le Viet Dung
Frances Lee
Emily Leinster
Sasha Leinster
Andrew Lewis
Sheldon Lewis
David Liddel
Ken Lieberman
Prasert Lipiwathana
Razzaq Lodhia
Ratanawalee Loharjun
Robyn Low
Nancy Madlin
Alfred Mandel
Nimit Maneekit
Richard Martin
Davis Masten
Lucienne & Richard Matthews
Margaret Maupin
Jon Mayes
Stewart McBride
Mike McConnell
Rob McHugh
Fiona McKaskie
Shawn McKee
Liz Perle McKenna
Laurie Mclean
Sam McMillan
Kevin McVea
Jim Melcher
Tom & Sharon Melcher
Brita Meng
Doug & Tereza Menuez
Joyce Meskis
Bill Messing

Jane Metcalf
Rand Miller
Robyn Miller
Clement Mok
Robin Moody
Frank Moore
Michael Moore
Richard Moore
Ron Moreau
Marney Morris
Ann Moscicki
Sue Moss
Walter Mossberg
Mike Muhlethaler
Steve Muir
Hank Nagashima
Vitayavanich Narong
Graham Nash
Hilary Nation
David Beffa Negrini
Doug Nelson
Grazia Neri
Nguyen Giang
Kimberly Nguyen
Nguyen Duy Anh
Nguyen Huy Phan
Nguyen Lan
Nguyen Minh Tri
Nguyen Quang Hung
Nguyen Thanh Long
Nguyen Thanh Minh
Nguyen Thi Phiet
Nguyen Thi Thom
Gerri Nietzel
Chris Noble
Chuck & Shirley Novak
Al Noyes
Catherine O'Brien
Rory O'Connor
Jimmy O'Donnell
Peg O'Donnell
Dan O'Shea
Karen Olcott
Paul Oliva
Laura Oliver
Gene Ostroff
Mark Ouimet
Michael Ovitz
Rusty Pallas
Andy Park
Maynard Parker
Amy Parrish
Sandra Patterson
James Paoletti
Anthony Paul
Daniel Paul
Scott Payne
Gabe Perle
John Perr
Ricardo Perran
Tom Peters
Pham Nhu'Anh
Pham Quang Loc
Pham Sy Toan
Pham Thi Hong Thanh
Phan Van Kinh
John & Janet Pierson
Alberto & Jennifer Pinto
Catherine Pledge
Robert Pledge
Ronald Pledge
Jenna Plumb

Len Polisar
Henri Poole
Elizabeth Pope
Cris & Ollie Popenoe
Richard Post
Karsten Prager
Tom Privitere
Michael Proulx
Larry Provost
Natasha & Jeff Pruss
Ruthann Quindlan
Bryant Rapolla
Peter Rattray
Nora Rawlinson
Betty Redmond
Eli Reed
Pamela Reed
Susan Reich
Kristin Reimer
Spencer Reiss
Michael Rex
Nick Rhodes
Doug Rice
Gail Rice
Peter Richards
Tom Rielly
Barbara Roberts
Jeffrey Roberts
Ty Roberts
Debbie Donnelly &
    Justin Robinson
Carol Rocco
John Rocco
Richard Rocco
Anita Roddick
David Rose
Jane & Peter Rosenthal
Bill & Faye Rosenzweig
Joe Roth
Richard RothHaas
Joe Runde
Brooke Runette
Kathy Ryan
Tom Ryder
Tom & Sondra Rykoff
Paul & Jennifer Saffo
Nola Safro
Sebastiao & Lelia Salgado
Marianne Samenko
Curt Sanburn
Will & Marta Sanburn
Pornpoj Santiluckana
H. Lockwood Saunders
Shekhar Sawant
Jamie Saxton
Murray & Jenny Sayle
Fred & Joanne Scherrer
Amy Schiffman
Aaron Schindler
Andreas Schläpfer
Jeff Schon
David Schonauer
Eric Schuman
Julie Schwerin
John Sculley
Lisa See
Tom Sellars
Jonathan Seybold
Harold Shain
Ira Shapiro
Ron Shapiro
Nathan Shedroff

Stephanie Sherman
Dale Shimono
Moe Shore
Eric Shropshire
Jane Sinclair
Kevin Sindelar
Aaron Singer
Bob Siroka
Richard Skeie
Brian Smiga
Jeffrey Smith
Martin Cruz Smith
Megan Smith
Rick Smith
Rodney Smith
Leslie Smolan
Marvin & Gloria Smolan
Sandy Smolan
Joy & Marty Solomon
Mike Solomon
Russ Solomon
Joe & Maura Sparks
Michael Spindler
Lisa Spivey
Alan Spoon
Ginny Stallard
Bruce Stanley
Adam Sternbach
Andy Stewart
Jim Stockton
Cliff Stoll
Dick Stolley
Jeff Stone
Linda Stone
Nancy Stone
Oliver Stone
Steve Stücky
Tak Sugiyama
Tony Sun
Peter Sutch
Linda Sutherland
Germaine Loc Swanson
Greg Swayne
Maurice Tani
Jay Tarrant
Michael Tchao
Michael Tette
Eugene Theroux
Paul Theroux
Carol & Chris Thomsen
Suwat Thongthanakul
Thuy Ha
Alexandra Todd
Tran Phuong
Tran Quoc Toan
Tran Van Luong
Joel B. Truher
Karen Tucker
Geoffrey Tudor
Mary Turnbull
Tony Turner
Dennis Urban
David Ushijima
Eric & Nina Utne
Michael van der Kieft
Della Van Heyst
Vuong Thinh
Barry Wain
Keith Walker
Wittaya Wong Wanich
Bill & Donna Warner
John & Marva Warnock

Jennifer Watanabe
Thomas Watson
Don Weinstein
Joshua Weisberg
Adele Weiss
Andrew Welch
Kevin Weldon
Albert Wen
Megan Wheeler
Scott Wiener
Sherri Wigger
Sanon Wilaiwongs
Harry Wilker
Dave Willard
David & Christine Williams
Preston & Dotty Williams
Robin & Marsha Williams
Mo Wilson

Ann Winblad
Dave Winer
Matt & Julie Winokur
Charlie Winton
Mike Winton
Jackson Wong
Janet Wong
Bob & Tone Woodhouse
Susan Woodrum
Bob Workman
Sam & Max Worrin
Simon Worrin
David Yakir
Tom Zazueta
Paul Zielbaur
Caren Zilber
Maurice & Barbara Zilber
Bertha Ziman

Passage to Vietnam was produced start to finish, in only twelve weeks. Many people wonder how a project like *Passage to Vietnam* is organized and how we were able to juggle the complex logistics involved in researching and coordinating assignments for 70 photographers throughout Vietnam, editing the 200,000 photographs they shot, designing and organizing the presentation of the final 180 images, and researching and writing captions and essays.

The key to this project was our use of Apple Computer's Macintosh cutting-edge desktop-publishing and related technologies. Each of our seventeen full-time staff members used a Powerbook 540C connected by a wireless infrared network system from Photonic Cooperatives, utilizing CE Software's QuickMail electronic mail system. Detailed research was facilitated with Dialog's online database using Global Village Mercury fax modems. Shiva's Lanrover/e modem allowed our traveling researchers to consult on-line with our offices in Singapore, California, Bangkok and Hanoi. Traveling staff used Technöggin's Powerplate 5X battery packs for long international flights and time in the field. America Online was used as a common E-mail system.

Assignment ideas were organized and logged in with Symantec's More 3.1 outlining program. The database and word processing modules of Clarisworks were used to keep track of photographers locations and to produce written descriptions for their Vietnam photo shoots.

The book was designed and produced on three Macintosh Quadra 840AV computers equipped with CD-ROM drives and 21" Supermac Supermatch PressView monitors. The Kodak slides were developed by A&I Color Laboratory and digitized by Zzyzx Visual Systems onto a series of Kodak PhotoCD discs. Flat artwork was scanned on an Apple Scanner using Light Source's Ofoto scanning software. Layouts were saved onto 150 megabyte Bernoulli cartridges. Images were color-corrected using Adobe Photoshop, assisted by Daystar's Photomatic software. Layout was done using Aldus PageMaker 5.0, with final assembly and linkage of the layouts stored on a Pinnacle 128 optical drive. We were able to initially proof the entire book at full size on a NewGen Systems 11"x17" 1200 DPI Imagesetter laser printer. We printed thumbnails of the book in color on a Xerox MajestiK copier driven by a Supermac Splash•MX Postscript enhancement card directly out of our Quadra 840 AVs. This allowed us to preview the entire book in color and show it to bookstore representatives many months ahead of publication.

Other software used in producing *Passage to Vietnam* included: Intuit's Quicken, Now Up-to-date and Now Contact, Kodak Access Software, CE Software's Quickkeys and Calendarmaker, Arrange from Common Knowledge, Virtus Walkthrough, Clinton by PF Bentley, Home Tool Kit from Books that Work, Cyan's Myst (Broderbund), The Rabbit & The Hare from Broderbund's Living Books series, and The Magic Death by Shannon Gilligan, courtesy of Creative Multimedia.

We gratefully acknowledge these companies for their generous support of *Passage to Vietnam*.

AGAINST ALL ODDS PRODUCTIONS

Passage to Vietnam
created and produced by:

Project Directors
Rick Smolan
Jennifer Erwitt

Managing Editor
Mark Rykoff

Writer
Colin Leinster

Production Coordinator
Denise Rocco

Production Associate
Gina Privitere

Assignment Editors
Bronwen Latimer
Lac Moreau
Michael Zilber

Researchers
Michael Zilber
John Darrah
Kieu-Linh Caroline Valverde

Research Consultant
Professor Truong Buu Lam,
   University of Hawaii

Additional Writing
Dana Sachs

Copy Editors
Elizabeth Leahy
Janice Maloney

Proofreader
Sheila Schat

Bangkok Liaison
Page N. Englehart

Hanoi Liaison
Suzanne Kauffman

Logisitics Coordinators, Hanoi
Gayle Driskell
Gene Driskell

Administrative Assistant
Casey Woodrum

PUBLICITY

Publicity Director
Patti Richards

Publicist
Gina Privitere

Publicity Consultants
Joan Rosenberg
Tricia Chan

DESIGN

Creative Director & Designer
Thomas K. Walker
   GRAF/x

Picture Editors
Woodfin Camp
   Woodfin Camp and Associates
Mike Davis
   National Geographic Magazine
Bill Douthitt
   National Geographic Magazine
Mary Dunn
   Entertainment Weekly
Colin Jacobson
   The Independent
Bronwen Latimer
Michele McNally
   Fortune
Mark Rykoff
Mike Smith
   Detroit Free Press
Michele Stephenson
   Time

Graphics Assistant
Duane Nelson

Map Illustrator
Martin S. Walz

ADMINISTRATION

Legal Services
Barry Reder,
   Coblentz, Cahen, McCabe & Breyer

Accounting
Gene Blumberg

Bookkeeper
Holly Bacuzzi

Travel Services
Barbara Henley
   Sunventure Travel
Nancy Nelson
   Sunventure Travel

Proposal Development
Tom Jacobs

Computer Consultant
Stephen Zilber

EDITIONS DIDIER MILLET

Co-Publisher, Singapore
   Publisher
   Didier Millet

   Managing Director
   Charles Orwin

   Editorial Director
   Peter Schoppert

   Project Consultant
   Marina Mahathir

   Media Director
   Yvan Van Outrive,
      ImMEDIAte Media

   Flight Liaison
   Irene Tan

MELCHER MEDIA

Co-Publisher, USA
   Publisher
   Charles Melcher

   Editorial Assistant
   Liza Siegler

THE MINISTRY OF CULTURE AND INFORMATION, HANOI
   Deputy Minister
   Nguyen Khoa Diem

   Deputy Director
   Pham Xuan Sinh

   General Manager
   Le Ngoc Thuy

   Liaison Officer
   Tran Thi Thuc

Television Production
REBO Group L.P.
   Barry Rebo
   Randy Bradley
   Kathy Scott
   Pat Weatherford
   Karen Mullarkey
   Barry Minnerly
   Abby Levine
   Steven Dupler
   Angel Annussek
   Khea Williams
   Clinton Cowles
   Raymond Campbell

FINANCE & DEVELOPMENT

Manager Smolan Millet

Legal Advisor
   F. Richard Pappas

Financial Advisor
William Osborne III,
   McKinley Capital Partners

Special Advisors
Sondhi Limpthongkul
   Manager Group
Ambassador Le V. Bang
   Socialist Republic of Vietnam
Chertchai Methanayaonda
   Thai Airways
Michael Magnus
   Magnus, Nankervis, Curl & Howard
Phillip Moffitt
   Light Source
Sheila Costello
   Eastman Kodak Company
Penny Post
   Vietnam Business Association
Wilson Tan
   Apple Computer
Tim Wheeler
   Apple Computer
Hugh Levin
   Lauter Levin Associates
Georgia McCabe
   Applied Graphics Technology
Scott Brownstein
   Applied Graphics Technology
Karen Mullarkey
   Talking Pictures

Printing and Separations
Palace Press International
   Gordon Goff
   Sales Manager
   Raoul Goff
   Production Director
   On-press Supervisor
   Greg Della Stua
   Production Manager
   Eric Ko
   Film Production Manager

Photo this page: Halong Bay. Photo by Gueorgui Pinkhassov, France
Pages 212-213: Ho Chi Minh City at night. Photo by Catherine Karnow, USA